"Randy J. Paterson has hit a home run with this highly accessible, engaging book. *How to Be Miserable* uses tongue-in-cheek humor, scientifically grounded practical advice, and a healthy dose of what is colloquially known as 'reverse psychology' to help put an end to common behavioral patterns that contribute to unhappiness. Anyone who wants to be less miserable should read this book and do the opposite of everything it recommends!"

> —**Martin M. Antony, PhD, ABPP**, professor of
> Mpsychology at Ryerson University in Toronto, ON,
> Canada, and coauthor of *The Shyness and Social
> Anxiety Workbook* and *The Anti-Anxiety Workbook*

"Randy J. Paterson's *How to Be Miserable* contains practical, witty, and wise advice, and is based on the premise that we have become our own worst enemies. Confronting our 'management' strategies consciously is the only way our life actually begins to turn toward better outcomes."

> —**James Hollis, PhD**, Jungian analyst, and author of
> *The Middle Passage* and *Finding Meaning in the Second
> Half of Life*

"Randy J. Paterson has failed miserably in his quest to create a recipe for unhappiness in *How to Be Miserable,* and instead has written a gem of a parody on how to cope with the inevitable difficulties we all must face in order to live a happy and fulfilling life."

> —**Simon A. Rego, PsyD, ABPP**, associate professor of clinical psychiatry and behavioral sciences at Albert Einstein College of Medicine/Montefiore Medical Center in New York, NY

"*How to Be Miserable* is a different kind of self-help book. By learning the forty traps that lead to unhappiness, readers will actually discover how to create the life they've always wanted—one filled with lasting happiness."

> —**Matt McKay, PhD**, coauthor of *Thoughts and Feelings*

HOW TO BE
Miserable

40 STRATEGIES YOU ALREADY USE

RANDY J. PATERSON, PhD

NEW HARBINGER PUBLICATIONS, INC.

Publisher's Note

This publication is designed to provide accurate and authoritative information in regard to the subject matter covered. It is sold with the understanding that the publisher is not engaged in rendering psychological, financial, legal, or other professional services. If expert assistance or counseling is needed, the services of a competent professional should be sought.

Distributed in Canada by Raincoast Books

Copyright © 2016 by Randy J. Paterson
New Harbinger Publications, Inc.
5674 Shattuck Avenue
Oakland, CA 94609
www.newharbinger.com

Cover design by Amy Shoup

Acquired by Melissa Kirk

Edited by Jennifer Eastman

Library of Congress Cataloging-in-Publication Data on file

Printed in the United States of America

18   17   16

10 9 8 7 6 5 4 3 2 1   First printing

For Benjamin

A pack of blessings lights upon thy back;

Happiness courts thee in her best array;

But, like a misbehaved and sullen wench,

Thou pout'st upon thy fortune and thy love:

Take heed, take heed, for such die miserable.

—Shakespeare, *Romeo and Juliet*

The greatest happiness is to know the source of unhappiness.

—Fyodor Dostoevsky

Contents

The Dreams of Another Age

Hundreds of self-help books are published every year. Each one, directly or indirectly, has the same purpose: how to make you happy. How to get rich so you'll be happy. How to be thin so you'll be happy. How to overcome depression so you'll be happy. How to find a relationship so you'll be happy. How to have high-colonic enemas so you'll be happy.

There is an irony in these extensive, groaning shelves. The very fact that there are so many of these books suggests that the target is extremely elusive—that happiness isn't easy.

Conjure in your mind the image of a caveman.

In your vision, he probably looks rather stupid. But he is us. Our species, *Homo sapiens sapiens,* has been around in pretty much the same form for over a hundred thousand years. And, stupid or not, our caveman has dreams. He longs for a world in which good-tasting food is readily available and starvation is unlikely. He wants freedom from the predators that occasionally make off with members of the tribe. He wants his children to stop dying from diseases he does not understand. When he is himself ill, he wishes that someone would help him get well.

Then he shakes his head, frowns at himself for wasting time, and returns to the business of survival. Pointless to wish for a world that could never exist.

But it can—and does.

In the developed world, we live a life of luxury unparalleled in the history of the species. There's food in the fridge, there's a roof over our heads, there's hot water in the faucet, there's hot air in our furnaces and leaders, and every product we can think of is within reach. We have a longer life span than ever. We're healthier for longer. The neighbors are not, for the most part, trying to kill us. The infant mortality rate is low, and the lifespan is long.

It is a world that our caveman, and the kings of not so very long ago, would quite happily have killed for (and one which the present-day citizens of many less privileged nations dream about). If we could reach back in time and bring our ancestors to the present world, their eyes would widen in amazement. We would show them our cars, our aircraft, our hospitals, our grocery stores, and the climate-controlled rooms where we sit in comfortable chairs to do our "work."

They would stare at us with a sudden realization. "I've died. This is the promised realm our priests talked about. Your days are spent in comfort and bliss. Can I stay?"

Then you tell them that there is a blight in this paradise. Most people are not filled with joy. Many spend much of their time in a state of dissatisfaction. Some are hospitalized in deepest misery. Millions are given medication to lift their moods to a tolerable level. Publishers bring out hundreds of books on how to find the happiness that microwave ovens and stable societies and Zumba classes have somehow failed to provide. Bus shelters advertise distant destinations to which the inhabitants of this world can escape.

Escape? Our caveman can think of nothing more wonderful than to be imprisoned here. He doesn't understand. He cannot.

Something has gone wrong.

THE TEN-MILLION-DOLLAR QUESTION

Misery sneaks up on you.

Many years ago, I was midway through my predoctoral internship in psychology when misery popped by for what turned out to be a yearlong visit.

At first I had no idea what was happening. I couldn't sleep, I couldn't eat, I could barely read a sentence, and a flight of stairs might just as well have been the Annapurna Circuit. Nothing appealed. At times, it seemed I could barely talk. Once, in a depressive fog, I greeted a new patient with the pronouncement, "This is Randy Paterson," causing the poor woman to peer around to see if I might be introducing her to someone more promising than I was.

A flippant list of a few symptoms does not serve to illuminate the sheer wretchedness of much of this period. I could go on, but let's leave that for another day.

I was *treating* depression, for goodness' sake, and still failed to notice it overtaking me. When I finally twigged, I was tempted to dismiss it. Young, healthy, pursuing a career I'd chosen at the age of eight—what did I have to be so unhappy about?

The answers, rolling their eyes, eventually tapped me on the shoulder, annoyed that I hadn't noticed them standing there.

Some were outside my control. The internship demanded long hours on multiple wards, seeing patients with both psychiatric and physical illnesses, many of the latter being terminal cases. One of my best friends at the time was dying. My internship was far from the friends I'd developed in graduate school, in a bedroom community known chiefly for the cheerful ease with which the residents had evacuated some years before, when a train carrying toxic chemicals derailed. (The miracle, so the local joke went, was not that everyone got out but that they ever returned.)

Some of the factors, however, were the result of my own choices. I didn't need to work quite as much as I did, and I was pushing myself in the evenings and on weekends to write my dissertation. I was drinking far too much coffee and eating too much gelatinous hospital food. I wasn't staying in contact with friends, seldom left my slum apartment (in a neighborhood that was red-circled by the social workers at the hospital), and got almost no exercise.

I scraped through, largely by fantasizing that I was my own patient and (mostly) following the standard recommendations. I exercised more, cut the coffee, took weekends off, ate better, made a point of seeing friends, and so on. Still, it took almost a year before I was back to what I usually considered my normal state.

After graduation, I specialized in the treatment of anxiety disorders, coyly shying away from seeing too much in the way of depression. A bit too close to home for comfort.

Homesick for mountains, I applied for every possible job on the West Coast and (fate having a delicious sense of humor) was offered a position as coordinator of a hospital-based mood disorder program. I accepted and, contrary to my own predictions, stayed there for nine years before opening a private clinic with a focus on—you can guess—mood problems. Our hospital team ran groups for people in the grip of more than just garden-variety misery. All had been hospitalized; most of them, several times. Their struggle easily dwarfed anything I had gone though. In my own cushioned life, I had visited the edge of the valley, but clearly had not dropped to its very bottom.

Early on, we began conducting a discussion exercise as part of the first session of the program. Our clients had been struggling to feel better for months—in some cases, for decades. They were understandably skeptical that anything we might do in our little group would be helpful. So we turned it around.

"Imagine that you could earn $10 million for just half an hour's work—let's say tomorrow morning between 11:00 and 11:30. All you would have to do is make yourself feel *worse* than you do now. Worse, in fact, than you've felt in the past week. How would you do it?"

Sometimes people would object, saying that it still wouldn't be worth the money or that they feared getting stuck there. One woman gazed balefully across the table at me. "So far, I have been doing this for *free*. Ten million? Fine."

What ensued, invariably, was a free-for-all of ideas that came haltingly at first and then in a flood. After one session, a hospital cleaner stopped in the hall as I was locking up and asked what had been going on in there. "Depression group," I said. "But they were laughing," she said, frowning. "You don't hear a lot of laughter in this building."

Each time we did the exercise, however, the humor would subside when I asked, "When you wake up in the morning, and you're already miserable, what do you feel like doing?" They would begin listing many of the same things that they had just nominated as strategies to feel worse.

"Why do you think that is?"

Some worried that perhaps they just liked being depressed. But this didn't fit. Of all the experiences they'd had, depression was almost always the most wretched. They didn't like it at all.

Misery changes everything. It affects how we feel, how we think, what we do—and it alters our impulses. When we are miserable, we are usually tempted to do precisely what, at other times, we know will make it worse. The result can be that we appear to be bringing on our own discomfort.

"In this group," I and the other leaders would say, "we're going to try to become aware of these impulses—and often we're going to try to do the opposite. Most of what we talk about won't seem tempting or promising or even logical. The strategies may feel wrong. But what feels right when you're miserable is what feeds the misery, not what feeds you."

Clinical depression, as should be obvious, is an extreme form of human misery. But there is no clear border dividing it from its milder cousins. Many of my present-day clients are less than happy about their lives, but not clinically depressed. Some arrive at my office doing just fine—but having heard about the new field of positive psychology, they wonder if they can go from tolerable or middling life satisfaction to better than average. Some of the strategies are unique to where a person starts out. Most are not.

We can learn from the answers given by the truly depressed to the Ten-Million-Dollar Question. Indeed, most of the strategies in this book first arose in those groups. You can ask the question of yourself. If you wanted to feel worse rather than better, what would you do?

This book, it must be noted, is not intended for those in the deepest valley of depression. At such a time, people often need other strategies and another voice. They may be put off by any chirpiness of tone. Instead, this book is for the larger population—those who have not fully explored the canyons of human emotion. Misery is a normal human experience. We all encounter it to varying degrees, and often we are surprised by its knock. So rather than waiting, let's open the door and set out to find it.

A misery safari. Pith helmets are optional.

COLUMN A AND COLUMN B

What causes a person's mood to rise or fall? Apart from mysterious fluctuations in the internal soup in which our brains simmer, what factors launch a person upward to the pinnacles of happiness or propel them to the valley floor?

We can divide the answers into two categories.

The first—let's call it Column A—comprises the inventory of catastrophe that can overtake us. Despite our privileged society, tragedy and disappointment still exist. Cars collide. Cells metastasize. Industries fail. Bodies age. Partners leave. Friends move. Roofs leak. Poverty and disease still thrive. We are not in full control of the circumstances of our lives. We can imagine that we have arranged our lives so carefully, with such foresight, that we have assured our happiness—and yet we know that circumstance can sweep it all away.

So there are limits to our personal influence. We can do all the right things and still get hit by a bus. If we are five feet tall, we can practice and perfect our basketball skills all we like, but we will still never play in the NBA. We can eat right, give up smoking, and take our vitamins, and we are still guaranteed to slip off the dish before our 120th birthday.

Life can impose a dizzying array of circumstances upon us that may limit our happiness or create misery: war, poverty, refugee status, personal misfortune of any stripe. You may be born with any of a variety of constraints—sensory, intellectual, social, familial. We can be fired, dumped, duped, flooded, infected, bombed, bullied, struck, abandoned, bankrupted, blind-sided, T-boned, or poisoned by an undercooked hamburger.

Some events, in retrospect, seem to have been so unlikely that it never occurred to you to worry about them. Just when my own life was going pretty well, I was shot off my bicycle by a deer that had been struck and air-launched by a passing vehicle. Sometimes it appears that fate has it in for you. I took my deer impact as a message from the fates to make some much-needed changes in my career. "Look what we can do! Get on with your life, or next time it'll be a moose."

In addition to these capricious whims of fate, however, there are many influences on our moods that lie within our own control. Let's put these in Column B.

We can choose what to eat, how to spend our time, how much exercise to get, and what to make priorities in our lives. All of these will influence—within the limits fate imposes upon us—how happy or miserable we become. We may not be able to live to be a thousand years old no matter what we do, but we can increase the likelihood of reaching a relatively healthy ninety. Whatever our lifespan, we can choose to spend our years isolated in front of a computer monitor or fully engaged with humanity and existence.

Even the factors outside our control may not impose limits that are as rigid as they appear. Some who have gone through horrific tribulations or who labor under what we might imagine to be intolerable circumstances are, despite it all, fairly happy. We might imagine that we could never again be upbeat if our partner left us or if we lost our job or if our home burned down. But read any number of biographies, and you find people who have gone through unimaginable losses and eventually returned to a full emotional life. We too may be surprised by joy just when all chance of it seems to have been extinguished.

So what's this book about? Well, there's no point in sitting in a field either summoning or attempting to avert an asteroid strike. The events of Column A are out of our control. We will take as given the fact that every one of us has circumstances that are immutable and unwelcome. Our efforts will instead focus on Column B: the mood-influencing factors that lie within the scope of our own choices. Within these pages, we will examine elements of life that can be controlled or selected, for good or ill.

There are many in the world who might look at the comfort, luxury, and leisure of life in developed countries and assume that misery would be impossible in such a place. Surely there is a lower limit to how awful a person can feel when the refrigerator is full. This appears not to be the case, however. As the data on life satisfaction, depression, and suicide all attest, no amount of wealth or good fortune can entirely prevent misery.

Our species has a talent for it.

WHAT'S THE PROBLEM?

Happiness seems like such a straightforward thing, and we appear to have every advantage that our ancestors might have asked for. Why are we so bad at achieving it?

One answer is the caveman himself. Our ancestors developed in a primitive, tribal world inherited from earlier hominid species—one that continued fairly well intact until not many thousands of years ago. Their bodies and their psychology were adapted to and shaped by that world. Take a fish, an admirably adapted creature, and plunk it in the desert; things will not go swimmingly. Take a hominid and plunk her in a vastly different world of computers, automobiles, television, and forty-hour workweeks, and she too has some difficulty adapting. The environment does not fit her nature.

"Oh, but wait," says the know-it-all in the back corner. "Our cave people *created* this modern world specifically based on hominid needs and psychology—so it should be perfectly matched to us."

This is not actually true, however. This world was created based on hominid *desires*, not on a dispassionate analysis of what might work best. Take creatures from a sugar-poor world who have consequently developed a powerful sweet tooth, and they will create a society of candy bars and soda pop. Because their bodies are not adapted to such an environment, they will have difficulty handling sudden sugar rushes, and they may exhibit a proneness to type 2 diabetes—as indeed has happened. The prevalence of seemingly inexplicable unhappiness may have a similar explanation. Our early surroundings have given us drives and instincts that, today, work against our best interests.

A related answer seems to lie within a peculiar wiring fault in humanity. As Daniel Gilbert so admirably described in his 2006 book, *Stumbling on Happiness*, human beings are remarkably poor at guessing what will make them happy in the future. Given that many of our decisions about present action are based on hypothesized future happiness, this means that we, as a species, constantly strike out confidently in precisely the wrong direction.

Yet another influence comes in the form of the messages we are given. In centuries past, we might learn much about life from the wisdom of our elders. Today, the majority of the messages we receive about how to live a good life come not from Granny's long experience of the world, but from advertising executives hoping to sell us products. If we are satisfied with our lives, we will not a feel a burning desire to purchase anything, and then the economy may collapse. But if we are unsatisfied, and any of the products we buy actually delivers the promised lasting fulfillment, subsequent sales figures may likewise drop.

We exist in a fog of messaging designed explicitly to influence our behavior. Not surprisingly, our behavior often shifts in precisely the manner intended. If you can be made to feel sufficiently inferior due to your yellowed teeth, perhaps you will rush to the pharmacy to purchase whitening strips. The lack of any research whatsoever correlating tooth shade with life satisfaction is never mentioned. Having been told one hundred times a day how to be happy, we spend much of our lives buying the necessary accoutrements and feeling disappointed not to discover life satisfaction inside the packaging.

LET'S ALL EMBRACE THE DARK SIDE

Between the influences of our culture, our physiology, and our psychology, it appears that striving for happiness is a tiring matter; we're swimming against a powerful current. We might almost say that happiness in such circumstances is *unnatural*.

If you are struggling through a wilderness and run up against an impenetrable wall, it only makes sense to look around and try the other direction. Given the thousands of books pointing toward happiness and their apparent lack of impact on global life satisfaction, perhaps we should turn our attention to the almost empty shelf nearby, the one reserved for guideposts to another destination: misery. If, in the presence of unparalleled wealth and privilege, we are capable of dissatisfaction, then perhaps misery is humanity's true signature strength. Let's optimize it.

This book, then, strikes off in the opposite direction to all those guides to the alleged good life. If we embrace misery as our goal, what is the path? Given the rarity of guides to this twilit land, one might think there would be little research to guide us. In fact, nothing could be further from the truth. Millions—perhaps billions—of dollars have been spent researching the question of how people become miserable. Today, if we want to be unhappy, we know how to bring it about. We have the technology.

Perhaps you are undecided about this quest. No matter. People buy travel guides all the time and never visit the regions covered. You need not sign a declaration in blood that you will commit to the path. But, in case one day you should choose this adventure, let's describe the route.

In *The Great Divorce*, C. S. Lewis (author of the Narnia books) describes a bus tour of heaven departing daily from the lower reaches of hell. Once there, the tourists are free to step off the bus and stay rather than returning, though few ultimately choose to do so. In this book, let us set off from the cave person's vision of heaven and visit hell instead. We'll explore the route and the signposts so you can find your way down anytime you like. Stay as long as you wish.

Of course, perhaps some days you are already there.

FOUR POINTS, FORTY LESSONS

Misery is not just a destination. It's a bit like tennis: a skill set that can be honed and perfected. In this book, you will learn a variety of strategies to become less happy. Along the way, you may discover that you have already mastered many of them and practice them regularly. But you can always get better—or perhaps I should say *worse*.

The techniques are grouped into four main sections. The first, "Adopting a Miserable Lifestyle," describes the basic features of a depressing existence: things you can do on a day-to-day basis to enhance your unhappiness.

The second section, "How to Think Like a Miserable Person," places you in an internal cinema and describes strategies for creating low mood via alterations in your thinking. Simply by working with the placement of your attention, you can create unhappiness no matter what your external circumstances might be. Think of it as a set of anti-mindfulness lessons.

The third section, "Hell Is Other People," describes how to maximize your own unhappiness through your relationships. Social interaction is one of the most complex aspects of being human, and so it is relatively easy to toss a few spanners into the works.

Finally, in "Living a Life Without Meaning," we take a broader view of human existence and ask how to steer the ship of life toward rockier shores. This section includes discussions of guiding principles and strategies to eradicate any sense of purpose from our lives.

Perhaps this all sounds quite daunting. The quest for misery can seem a lonely one—a solitary, quixotic journey into an unexplored wilderness, leaving behind all that we have known.

Nonsense.

In a world where so many are unhappy with their lot, our culture has created a well-signposted superhighway to misery that all may travel, and that, one way or another, most do. This autobahn is the smoother path, and it has innumerable on-ramps, no speed limit, and multiple lanes. It is the road to happiness that is individual, weed-strewn, and overgrown from disuse.

Most of the lessons to come will sound familiar. Many are maxims you have heard all your life—though to sweeten them they have been touted as routes to fulfillment. So rest easy. As you walk this path, you will be surrounded by millions, and your culture will line the route, cheering you on.

Climb aboard; we are about to depart. I will be happy to serve as your tour guide to hell. I've been there before. Just follow my umbrella; I'll hold it aloft as I march on ahead.

I don't have $10 million to offer you.

But hey: So far you've been doing this for free.

A NOTE TO THE UNCOMMITTED

Every riverside path goes in both directions. Perhaps you are not committed to the downstream route—misery—which is where the rest of us are headed. Instead, you still want to go against the current in the opposite direction. Well, fine.

There is a rearview mirror installed in our tour bus, and along the way you can look at it as much as you wish. Listen closely to your guide. If, like your fellow riders, you want to embrace your unhappiness, follow the instructions given. If you secretly hope for the bus going the other way, simply do the reverse of what you are told.

Spoilsport.

PART ONE

Adopting a Miserable Lifestyle

What a miserable thing life is: you're living in clover, only the clover isn't good enough.

—Bertolt Brecht

When I first see someone who is alarmed by a prolonged period of low mood, I generally complete a full assessment. I find out about the person's overall health, recent traumatic events, and life history and upbringing. I ask about each of the diagnostic criteria for the depressive disorders. A first appointment with me is something of a cross between a chat over tea and a CIA interrogation.

Toward the end of the session, I often shift gears. "William, I'd like you to imagine for a moment that we go outside and grab the next twelve people who pass by this building. We're going to give them your life. Your sleep schedule. Your level of exercise. Your diet. Your amount of social contact. We'll give them your job, your boss, your home, your family, your financial situation—everything. Twenty-four hours a day, we'll have them live exactly the way you've been living recently. After a month we'll come back and see how they're doing. How do you think they'd be?"

William, a bit disoriented to discover that he's consulting a madman, blinks a bit. Then—whether his name is William or Johanna or Kamal or Carmelita—the reply is almost always the same: "I think they'd be depressed." Usually I agree.

Notice what I don't do. I don't give our abductees William's childhood history or losses or any of the other factors that might be involved in the development of his low mood. I just give them the life he leads now. Usually that's enough to make his present mood understandable. Sometimes I have to throw in, "And we'll have them think the way you think." At that point, he is all but certain to agree that the mood makes perfect sense. More often, however, giving our captives his behavior is enough.

Does this mean that none of those other causes of the low mood are relevant? Of course not. The near-drowning incident when he was eleven and the bullying he experienced all through high school are still with him. The divorce last year, his diabetes diagnosis, and the home invasion six months ago are profound influences. They will have to be dealt with. But they led him to adopt a way of living that now, alone, is sufficient to keep the fire burning. If all I do is focus on his history and ignore his current lifestyle, we will get nowhere. I will be fighting a forest fire by trying to track down the careless campers who started it—useful, perhaps, but insufficient.

If William is so displeased by his present mood, why does he not simply change his behavior? The answer lies in the interconnections between mood and impulse. As the mood darkens, the natural tendency is to withdraw and self-protect, conserving energy as we retreat into the depths of the cave to recover. William is doing what feels natural to him—so much so that it seems impossible for him to do anything else.

Causality, in this instance, travels in both directions. In order for our mood to become like William's, we do not need the divorce, the bullying, the home invasion, or the diabetes. All we need is to adopt his lifestyle. Misery is not out of reach for even the most fortunate among us. Let's consider ten of the most useful strategies.

LESSON 1

Avoid All Exercise

There is a firm tradition when writing a book of useful life tips. The author starts out with minor points and gradually builds toward more powerful ones. Partly this is a trick to keep the reader engaged out of pure suspense. But in this somewhat perverse volume, let's perversely do the opposite.

Imagine that someone announced that she wanted to lower her mood, but that forty changes seemed far too many. What if she were only willing to try ten—which ten would be most effective? What if she were willing to make only five changes? Three? What if she were only willing to change one thing? In that case, the choice would be simple. To increase your level of misery, reduce your level of exercise.

Of course, this recommendation is problematic, because for many who live in developed societies, it is all but impossible to carry out. The average citizen's level of exertion is already about as low as it can possibly get without outright paralysis. Teenagers complain of cramps if forced to walk to the convenience store. Thirty-year-olds pause for breath halfway up a flight of stairs. Forty-year-olds circle parking lots like descending Airbuses, searching for a space ten yards closer to the donut shop.

The low level of physical fitness probably accounts for a great deal of the preexisting misery in Western societies. It may not have been pleasant for cave people to be chased by saber-toothed tigers, but at least it gave them an occasional workout.

Nevertheless, for those whose lifestyle involves sufficient activity to set off a motion detector now and then, reducing the amount of exercise is a sound strategy. There is a huge body of evidence linking inactivity to lower mood.

Helpful researchers have examined the issue from all angles. When people are tested for both physical fitness and mood, an inverse relationship between the two is typically found. Especially unhappy individuals—those diagnosed with clinical depression—are, on average, less physically fit than their more cheerful counterparts.

Clever misery-seekers will point out a snag with this research—the chicken-and-egg problem. Are sedentary people more miserable, or do the miserable exercise less? The correct answer, it appears, is *both*. This makes the avoidance of exercise particularly potent. Do less exercise and your mood will decline, resulting in a greater tendency to be inactive. If you can success-fully initiate just a few vicious circles like this one, you will be well on your way to unhappiness.

Still not convinced? Take active individuals and reduce their level of exercise. Within as little as two weeks, fatigue and negative mood begin to set in.[1] Take unhappy individuals and randomly assign them to exercise classes (thirty minutes, three times a week) or no such classes.[2] On average, the exercisers will experience a loss of misery, whereas their inactive associates conserve it. The mood-raising effect of exercise is approximately as powerful as medication or psychotherapy. Those wishing greater unhappiness in their lives, then, must avoid physical fitness at all costs.

Luckily, all of Western society is there to help. In previous eras you would inadvertently get exercise by doing almost anything—running after buffalo, harvesting rice, gathering firewood, avoiding hostile neighbors. Today we have built a culture in which exercise is nonessential and even inconvenient. You seldom have to lift or carry anything of any weight, you need never walk more than a city block, and elevators (essentially forklifts for humans) can take you to any floor of any building you enter.

Today, people who want to be more fit often find that they have to drive to a business specially devoted to that purpose, change their clothes, get on special exercise machines that accomplish nothing other than help the inert burn energy, change their clothes again, and drive home. Some gyms have escalators, so you needn't exhaust yourself climbing any stairs before you arrive at the StairMaster.

Of course, anyone who watches late-night television will know that gyms are not essential; one can simply purchase cheaply built home exercise equipment. This is easily avoided, but if you one day awaken and discover with alarm that you or a well-meaning friend has ordered such a device, all is not lost. Just do what almost everyone else does. Hang a piece of clothing on it. Henceforth it is unlikely to be used for anything else.

The only caution about exercise is that it must be avoided religiously. As noted in the above studies, just thirty minutes of exercise three times per week is sufficient to disrupt unhappiness in most people. And exercise beyond this level is even worse. So it is not sufficient just to let your gym membership lapse. You must be more diligent:

- Drive wherever you go, even when walking might ultimately be faster.

- Aim to spend at least twice us much time on your posterior as you do on your feet.

- Purchase a pedometer and aim to end the day having taken less than a thousand steps.

- Select leisure activities (and professions) for their sedentary qualities. Web surfing is good; surfboarding is bad. Desk work serves your purpose; real work defeats it.

The unhappy heart is a fragile organ. It must never be permitted to pump rapidly.

Eat What You're Told

The human body is an immensely complex device. Like most machines, it requires a variety of supplies to maintain it. It needs fuel, obviously, either in the form of simple sugars or complex carbohydrates. It also needs fats, protein, and an elaborate stew of amino acids and minerals. Given a deficiency—or an excess—of one sort or another, a variety of things can happen. Among them is the induction or magnification of misery.

It can sound almost impossible to get one's body perfectly balanced—and therefore trivially simple to stir disorder and chaos. In the primitive environments in which the body evolved, however, the diet was enormously variable. One day antelope, the next day nuts. One could not supplement a meal of berries simply by swallowing a daily Senior VitaPack 50 Plus pill or ordering a macrobiotic smoothie at the juice bar. We adapted by developing the capacity to store many nutrients and by using cell walls that select what they need from the bloodstream and mostly ignore everything else. As a result, it can be more difficult than you might think to produce an imbalance.

Our challenging early environment did help us in one way, however. It left us with taste cravings. Certain nutrients, like salt, were somewhat hard to come by in times past. Nature compensated by providing us with a powerful drive to search out and ingest those substances. If they were lying around, we'd definitely want some rather than leaving it behind when the tribe moved on. "Skim milk yogurt? Umm, no, but do we have any of that salty boar's blood?"

Enter modern agriculture. When our society developed sufficiently that we could create a reliable supply of any nutrient we could want, these scarcity-bound tastes began to lead us astray. Today we turn our noses up at much-needed sources of potassium but gobble down as much sugar, salt, and fat as we can get our hands on.

If, in our culture of plenty, we obey our primitive impulses, we are likely to ingest a diet that will naturally produce difficulties, some of which will be emotional. With bodies designed for feast and famine, we will usually overeat when food is available and store the nonessential calories as fat. And obesity is linked directly to lower mood—and indirectly to misery-inducing problems, including inactivity, heart disease, and diabetes.

It can sound like hard work to overeat enough to cause problems. It isn't. Simply adding a single can of soda to your diet (or an equivalent amount of fruit juice) will give you about ten teaspoons of sugar per day—twice the World Health Organization's recommended daily intake. This will provide you with forty-seven thousand sugar-based calories in a year—the equivalent of about thirteen pounds of fat.

In addition, certain dietary deficiencies have been linked (though, in most cases, not conclusively) to reduced energy and mood:

- Many of the B vitamins, particularly B6 (pyridoxine), B9 (folic acid), and B12 (cobalamin).

- Vitamin D (though it must be added that most of the body's D is produced by sun exposure).

- Omega-3 fatty acids. The research isn't firm on the matter, but it suggests a link between deficiency and lower mood.

- Iron. Deficiencies are most likely to appear in women, vegetarians, and athletes.

Avoiding foods containing these nutrients may result not only in lowered mood but in reduced overall health as well.

Almost everything the body needs is readily available at the local supermarket. The very fact that we need it, however, means that it has been around too long to be patented. No one has a corner on the market for broccoli, so there is no incentive to advertise it. Instead, we have a wide variety of products cobbled together from processed ingredients and chemical additives, specially engineered to suit a cave person's urges. The recipes for these concoctions are proprietary, so companies stand to make a lot of money if they can create an awareness of and craving for the taste of their own specific products.

Consequently, you have an unintentional ally in your quest to lower your mood: the advertising industry. Simply place a notepad by your television, jot down all the products advertised, and use this as your weekly shopping list. Buy these, and you will be imbalanced, mentally and physically, within weeks. Further, you will be well on your way to a lifetime of impairments. Eat what they tell you.

If some crazed family member drags you off one day to a farmer's market or a natural-food store or starts ranting on about the Mediterranean diet, resist with vigor. Remind yourself that these foods were, not too long ago, sitting in dirt, growing in dirt, or covered with dirt. Remember what Mom told you: don't put dirty things in your mouth. Ensure that your diet comes out of a box instead—and that the box comes from a nice clean factory.

Don't Waste Your Life in Bed

The most valuable resource you have is time. No matter what you do, how much you earn, where you live, or how powerful you are, you get only 168 hours in a week. If you listen to the health purists, however, you will spend at least a third of those hours unconscious. People keep telling us that life is short, but then they seem to want to make it even shorter.

Instead, cast off the tyranny of slumber. Get by with as few hours of sleep as possible. As the wise say, there'll be plenty of time for sleep when we're dead.

This approach will aid us in our misery mission. By reducing our hours of restorative sleep, we will reduce our concentration, dull our mood, and become easily overwhelmed by life's demands. We will be more irritable, less productive, less creative, and more prone to bad decision making.

You don't have to sit around waiting for insomnia to strike. You can induce artificial insomnia simply by not giving yourself enough time to rest. Tell yourself that you are just too busy to loaf around in bed. If this isn't precisely true when you start out, it will soon become true. Your efficiency will drop as you become more sleep-deprived, and you will begin falling inexorably behind in the tasks of your work and your life.

Don't have the willpower for this? No problem. Disrupt your sleep more naturally. First, design your bedroom to promote sleeplessness:

- Buy a cheaper and less comfortable mattress than you can afford.

- Keep the room too warm.

- Ensure that intermittent noises from phones, e-mail alerts, and pets happen throughout the night.

- Have as many flashing LEDs on the walls and ceiling as you can manage. (Ask any hotel designer for advice on this one.)

- Buy a brightly glowing digital clock and aim it directly at your pillow, so you will see it and count the minutes all night.

- Ensure that your curtains are sheer enough to allow in light from the street. Complete darkness will only promote sleep.

When should you go to bed? A regular twenty-four-hour sleep-wake cycle takes most people three to four days to establish, so ensure that you vary your bedtime and rising time by at least a few hours every few days. Stay up three hours later on days when you don't have to go to work. Can't afford to travel enough to give yourself constant jet lag? No problem. This alone will do the trick, and without even leaving home!

Regardless of when you go to bed, spend that final hour on activities that ensure you don't drop off to sleep:

- Perform mentally difficult work.

- Watch the news.

- Read gripping novels that you will be unable to put down.

- Use your bedroom as a study space, workspace, dining area, television room, and for as many other activities as possible.

When you do eventually hit the sheets, make wise use of the wakeful time before you drift off. Worry. Think about your schedule and the difficulties likely to arise tomorrow. Consider your life in a broader context, and all the problems you are unlikely ever to solve. The result will be a significant delay in sleep onset. When you wake in the middle of the night, immediately focus your mind on problems and challenges. This should ensure that you don't go quickly back to sleep.

If the goal is to get fewer hours of restorative sleep, you should avoid sleeping in late, right? Wrong. Tell yourself you're going to "catch up on your sleep," and stay in bed. Altering your rising time appears to be even more effective at impairing sleep than randomizing your bedtime. So lie in bed until noon. You will only drift in and out of rapid-eye-movement (REM) sleep, and this doesn't generally make you feel any more rested. In fact, some research suggests that unrestricted REM sleep promotes a lowering of mood.

Ultimately you will want to create a self-perpetuating cycle of sleeplessness. There is a lovely trick for this. Once you have succeeded in creating at least a bit of sleep disruption, use your wakeful time to dwell on how important it is for you to get to sleep. Look at the clock and calculate how many hours remain before you have to get up. Tell yourself that tomorrow you will desperately need to be rested, and that time is slipping away. Ignore the fact that you have survived past sleepless nights and that trying to force yourself to sleep is the best way to stay awake. Jettison any sense of equanimity and replace it with stressed-out urgency. This should allow you to lie there wide-eyed and alert until dawn.

Finally, nap all you like. The thirty- to forty-five-minute "power nap" tends to be restorative for most people, so instead you will want the two-hour (or longer) "misery nap" that occupies much of the afternoon. This will leave you feeling groggy and unproductive, and it will make it even easier for you to lie in bed sleepless later that evening.

LESSON 4

Live Better Through Chemistry

One of the great paradoxes about lowering your mood is that it often works best to strike out in the direction of happiness rather than aiming straight at misery. The quest for uplift often hides a stairway leading sharply downward.

The use of a chemical assist to raise one's mood is a classic example. People drink alcohol, smoke pot, and practice other forms of "informal pharmacy" largely to elevate the mood. In the short term, these substances often perform precisely as advertised. In the long run, however, the diligent user can reap a substantial harvest in unhappiness.

Despite our culture's tendency to cluck disapprovingly about self-medication to alter mood, the most widely used drug is both legal and socially acceptable: alcohol. It causes more deaths (both directly, via organ damage, and indirectly, through traffic fatalities and other mishaps) than any other drug of abuse. Population-wide, it also creates the most misery. Moderate consumption of one to two drinks per day, however, appears to be relatively benign for most people. This is unlikely to assist you to your goal unless you have a familial vulnerability to alcohol dependence, in which case any use at all can help you find the fabled slippery slope.

For the maximum effect, you will want to drink more than a glass of wine with dinner. Alcohol is a depressant, so even if it affects no other aspect of your life, it will insidiously begin downshifting your mood. Two methods seem to be employed most often:

1. a steady pattern of daily or near-daily drinking that gradually ramps up to enormous proportions

2. an alternating pattern of moderation or abstinence interspersed with out-of-control binges

Either of these strategies will work, though the former is somewhat more likely to have the added effect of physical dependence, which will make withdrawal a misery as well.

The overuse of alcohol can have an impact on all areas of your life. For example, it tends to anaesthetize the inhibitory pathways of the brain. This is one of its biggest attractions for the shy. They can relax, open up, converse more easily, and drop rigid boundaries (and sometimes clothes). The hidden benefit for our purposes is that inhibition is critically important for proper functioning in social settings. We may feel tempted to make fun of a friend's outfit or political opinions, but normally we refrain from doing so. With overuse—and it's always difficult to calcu-late the ideal dose *just so*—alcohol will take the brakes off the mouth, allowing us to careen downhill into the realm of the social pariah.

Further, alcohol reduces the capacity for self-reflection. Under its influence, we may think we are performing well at work, being funny at a party, and driving with perfect skill—but we're not. One of the reasons that people are not more miserable than they are is that, sober, they instinctively respond to feed-back and hold themselves back when they see they are coloring outside the lines. Given enough alcohol, however, we can no longer detect the lines and so push fearlessly beyond them.

Longer term, the pinball of alcohol dependence can carom off of any of life's surfaces, intensifying and accelerating at every step. It can impair career success, friendships, marriages, child raising, the deeper stages of sleep, finances, and almost any other aspect of an otherwise-fulfilling life.

What about other drugs? This book is far too brief to describe the myriad downward possibilities offered by each sub-stance on the prohibition list. Broadly speaking, however, the pattern is similar to that for alcohol—with the added bonus of illegality and all of the fun and consequences that can bring.

There is one more substance worth considering, however, and it is again a legal one: caffeine. Sharp observers in North America have noted the increase in urban coffee shop density over the past few decades, concluding that if the pace continues there will be no room for any other form of business within twenty years.

Caffeine can trigger a stress response with the attendant fight-or-flight flavors of unhappiness: anger and anxiety. Small doses, for most people, do not seem significant and may only serve to sharpen concentration and motivation. But once one graduates to a more heroic habit (as little as three cups of drip coffee per day), anxiety, anger, or both are likely to be accentuated. You may even be able to trigger panic attacks or outbursts of rage. More often, you will experience a grinding uneasiness and irritability.

Plus, if you drink enough—of either coffee or alcohol—you will always have to be within 150 yards of a bathroom.

LESSON 5

Maximize Your Screen Time

Sometimes reducing one's mood is an active process. More often it is essentially passive: a matter of *not* doing things. The question, of course, is what to do instead. Simply sitting still is boring and hard to maintain. Mindfulness meditation may make you less miserable rather than more. You need an alternative. Fortunately, vast media industries have arisen to help occupy your mind while time slips away.

Consider television. The citizens of most Western countries spend significantly more time watching their screens than interacting with their partners, friends, or children. Smoking, it is said, shrinks the average person's life expectancy by ten years. But why stop there? Spending thirty-four hours per week watching television (the United States average) will occupy fully 30 percent of your waking hours—twenty-three years of the average person's conscious lifespan. This sounds intolerably dull, but viewing can become habitual, nibbling away at your life until you believe wholeheartedly that you do not have time for any of the things that might lift your mood: learning, reading, exercising, contributing to your community, seeing friends and family, cooking, or cultivating your interests and hobbies.

If you spend eight hours a night in bed, you have 112 waking hours a week. Spend thirty-four of them watching television, and you still have seventy-eight hours left that might inadvertently improve your life satisfaction. If you cannot bear another reality show, an alternative readily presents itself: the Internet. The average American usage is twenty-six hours per week or higher, depending on the study. Most surveys explicitly exclude Internet usage that is a part of paid employment, so the vast majority of those hours are voluntary.

How should you spend your time online? Surely you do not need advice on this front, but here are some options:

- Read the news in endless and irrelevant detail. Tell yourself you are enriching your life by learning about Belgian political sex scandals.

- Update social media with important information about your life—what you had for lunch, the flu symptoms you had yesterday—and share the adorable cat video someone posted earlier.

- Surf randomly from page to page, chasing forgotten tidbits of information, like the names of cast members from *Eight is Enough* or the date that Dynel was first patented.

- Watch video ephemera, like "Off-duty Marine unit demonstrates 'twerking' to Britney hit!" and

"Out-of-work actor creates claymation comedy using spray cheese."

- Marvel at (and add to) the inane and misspelled commentary on all of the above.

And—come on—much, much more.

Now then: fifty-two hours a week remain. How about computer gaming? Now a bigger moneymaker than the film industry, gaming occupies an average of thirteen hours a week for Americans twelve to twenty-four years of age. "Extreme gamers," about 4 percent of the gaming population, spend forty-eight or more hours per week.[3] Gaming is growing in popularity, and larger game-design firms employ experts whose primary role is to figure out how to get more women, young children, and older people to spend their lives shooting at other people's online avatars. Many people would not accept a job with such long hours as hard-core gamers are willing to put in.

At one point, it was believed that newer media would simply supplant older forms of electronic entertainment, taking over the time that people used to spend staring at *Bewitched*. But no. Television watching has remained relatively robust, particularly if one includes the viewing of the same programs online. Gaming and the Internet have not eaten television; they have instead consumed people's social lives, shared meals, and time spent out of doors. In Canada, spaces at limited-access wilderness areas are easier to get each year, perhaps because it is so difficult to play *World of Warcraft* in a canoe.

Total it up: fifty-two hours minus thirteen makes thirty-nine hours. Add a job, and we have successfully eliminated all unpaid conscious hours from your life. Is there a risk of fulfillment here? Apparently not. There are no studies indicating that gaming, Internet surfing, or television are, on balance, mood-improvers. To walk the path of misery, it turns out that walking isn't required at all. One must merely sit, spellbound, before a flickering screen that feels so important, so encompassing, that you simply do not have space in your life for anything else.

Take some time to calculate your weekly leisure screen-time ratio. It's easy to do. Simply add up your screen time (Television + Non-work Internet + Gaming), all divided by your hours of unpaid consciousness (168 hours in a week, minus the hours you spend in bed or at work). Let's say you watch television 3 hours a day, surf 2.5 hours a day, spend 2 hours a week playing computer solitaire, lie in bed 8 hours a day, and work 40 hours a week. This amounts to $((3x7) + (2.5x7) + 2)/(168—((8x7) + 40)) = 40.5$ hours of screen time / 72 non-work waking hours = 0.563, or 56.3 percent of leisure time spent on screens. Not bad, but this still leaves you with 31.5 hours a week of non-screen leisure. Bump up your television and Internet just to the US average, and this will get you to 62 hours, leaving virtually no time for anything at all that might inadvertently boost your mood.

What could be easier?

LESSON 6

If You Want It, Buy It

If you pay close attention to consumer advertising, it is easy to detect a theme: purchasing is the road to happiness. By this reasoning, it would be easy to conclude that a simpler, less object-heavy lifestyle is the correct path to misery.

This would be an error.

In fact, the key to misery is to avoid accidentally treading the path to fulfillment, and one of the best ways to accomplish this is to occupy one's time (and wallet) with the pursuit of objects. In this quest, your human mind will happily collude. Simply pay attention to the wonders paraded before you by the advertising industry and displayed beautifully in the shops that line your town's streets and malls. Your heart will learn to leap like a dog offered cheese. That sweater! That riding mower! That designer perfume! That barbecue with the six-foot rotisserie! You'll want it all.

The result of our society's consumer gluttony? If you thought, a decade ago, that investing in the personal storage industry would be a good bet, you were right. Storage units, once the curious domain of wealthy hoarders, have become mainstream.

Having filled their homes with things they do not need, people in Western societies have increasingly turned to outside suppliers of square footage where they can put all of their unused treasures. There is over 2.3 billion square feet of self-storage area in the United States alone, equivalent to more than three times the total area of Manhattan.

Why do we buy so much? The act of obtaining possessions usually reveals a person's implicit map to happiness:

"If I buy this inflatable boat, I'll go to the lake more often,

and I'll take my daughter with me fishing,

and we will have a better relationship,

and then I'll be happy."

And, sure enough, most people can point to specific objects they own that give them pleasure—as well as many that do not. In my case, $600 impulsively spent on a couch for my home office, where I imagined I would lie on summer afternoons reading Proust, was essentially flushed away, but the $20 paid for used truck tubes on which to float down a nearby river was eminently well spent.

The problem is not so much the purchasing itself, but the predictions we make. It is unlikely that most of the objects finding their way into storage units are the source of great personal pleasure. And humans are poorly wired to guess correctly.

As discussed earlier, in *Stumbling on Happiness*, psychologist Daniel Gilbert points out that (apart from purchasers of the book you're reading) humans generally base decisions about their behavior on the likelihood that their actions will bring pleasure in the future. Unfortunately, we are startlingly poor at making these predictions. Most Mercedes sedans are purchased not for the glories of German engineering, but for the mood that the buyer imagines will ensue—and its longevity. "It costs $80,000, but it will make me truly happy, and I'll probably have the car for eight years—so about $10,000 a year for a happy life, which seems reasonable."

The lovely thing about predictions like this is that they are completely testable. "How happy do you think it will make you? Okay, now go on and buy it, and let's see what happens." In many of these studies, it turns out that people become about as happy as they imagined. In other words, they guessed correctly. But the elevated mood lasts only a short time—sometimes a week, sometimes much less, depending on the purchase. Suddenly, $80,000 for a week's pride of ownership doesn't seem like such a bargain.

Swiss-British author Alain de Botton, in *Status Anxiety*, writes, "The best way to stop appreciating something is to buy it." (After I relayed this observation at a recent workshop, one of the female participants was heard to mutter, "or marry it.") De Botton seems to be right. A painting appreciated and admired out there in the world can be an object of pleasure and longing forever, but purchased and hung in one's front hall, it quickly becomes an ignored dust-collector.

The key point, for our purposes, is that the futile quest for emotional fulfillment via the purchase of objects is an excellent strategy for the longer-term cultivation of misery. What could be better than a constantly renewable pursuit that ends, again and again, in disappointment? Consumerism is even better than that might imply, however, because it also involves the outflow of money and resources. We strive to obtain the trappings of wealth and end up poorer than when we started. Perfect!

LESSON 7

Can't Afford It?
Get It Anyway!

One path to misery was laid out over 150 years ago by the improvident Mr. Micawber in Charles Dickens's *David Copperfield*: simply spend more than you earn. "Annual income twenty pounds, annual expenditure nineteen nineteen six, result happiness. Annual income twenty pounds, annual expenditure twenty pounds ought and six, result misery."

Some years back, a client in significant financial difficulty told me of the indecision she was experiencing after seeing something she wanted at the local mall. "I've got $500," she said, uncertain whether to make the purchase.

My instant thought was that spending money with only $500 in life savings was perhaps unwise, but I had misunderstood things completely. It turned out that she had no money at all, but on one of her credit cards, she had $500 remaining on her limit. Her personal balance sheet was not $500 up, it was many thousands down—and she was contemplating the wisdom of lowering it further. As the son of a Scottish accountant (in this case, all relevant stereotypes apply), it took all I had to avoid crying out in alarm.

I should explain. It was not this client's goal to feel worse, and a great part of her anxiety was caused by her financial situation and a sense that, as a result, she lacked the freedom to maneuver in her life—change her job, move apartments, travel, respond to emergencies. Her credit cards were handcuffs. For the person striving to feel worse, credit is one of the primary freeways leading there.

It is widely believed that money cannot buy happiness, but lack of money can definitely purchase misery. This can be true even if a person lives in relative comfort, with a good home and assured access to food and other resources. As one gets closer and closer to the financial wire, misery-inducing stresses proliferate:

- difficulty paying the bills

- phone calls from creditors

- having to cut back on basics

Perhaps the greatest stressor is the sense of impending doom—that, no matter how pleasant one's current circumstances may be, at any moment they could be swept away.

Money may not be able to buy happiness, at least not directly. But it can certainly buy freedom from fears of financial ruin.

Imagine yourself perched on a branch dangling over a rushing river. A vision of fulfillment rests gently on the far tip of the limb, over the deepest part of the torrent. Hypnotized, you inch yourself further and further out, hearing creaks and small snaps as you go. You are perfectly dry, and it is a warm, sunny day. The misery that overtakes you is the awareness of what may shortly happen.

Another client sought out therapy during a long period of unemployment following an unceremonious firing. He soon worked wonders on himself and landed an executive position with a prominent firm. After several months at this job, he commented that he was now making so much money that he didn't know what to do with it.

The best advice depends, of course, on the direction a person wants to pursue. In his case, it was to be happier and more secure. "Don't feel rich," I told him. His unemployment had exhausted his savings, and he lacked one of life's great bulwarks against work-related anxiety: enough funds to last at least six months with zero income. Following the lyrics of a popular country song addressed to an unpleasant employer, this is commonly called "take this job and shove it" money.

Had my client been an aficionado of the course upon which you, dear reader, are embarked, the advice would have been very different. "Assume that your future income will match or exceed your present income and spend accordingly, or a little bit more.

Assume debts, get your credit limit raised, and then use it—that's what it's for." Even with a high income and a good job, misery will likely ensue. Debt is an indispensible tool in the production of unhappiness.

"But wait," I hear you protesting. "I'm not just going to toss money from the rooftops, I'm going to buy things I really desire. Won't the pain of ongoing debt be assuaged by the joy of acquisition?" It certainly will—but only briefly. Debt, like diamonds, can be forever. It is the gift that keeps on taking.

Give 100 Percent to Your Work

Anthropologists estimate that nomadic cave people had a significant advantage over the civilizations that came after them: they worked perhaps four hours per day. Many people assume that agriculture developed because it was easier simply to sit still and watch plants grow than to traipse around looking for food that grew spontaneously. Not so. Agriculture increased the workload immensely.

Today, in developed societies, the workday is not quite so onerous as it was for early farmers or for workers during the Industrial Revolution. But it still vastly exceeds that for hunter-gatherer humans. The form of the work has also changed. If we put on our rose-tinted glasses, we can say that modern work is generally cleaner, safer, and easier than scavenging for meals. But donning our blue lenses, we can say that most work has lost its obvious connection to existence: we shuffle bits of paper, move objects around, type on keyboards, and create unnecessary products.

In *The Pleasures and Sorrows of Work*, Alain de Botton writes that the modern workplace subdivides tasks so much that each employee works on only a tiny bit of the process, rarely seeing a product or project from inception to completion.[4] He suggests, echoing Karl Marx, that this fragmentation can create an alienation from the work itself. Few of us would prefer to return to feudal farm life or resurrect the occupational glories of the Eastern Bloc, but the point is, for many, a valid one. It is somewhat more difficult to bask in a glow of achievement gazing at a pile of completed paperwork than when hammering the final nail into a freshly built barn.

Despite concerns about modern work and workplaces that are too numerous to mention, there is a constantly repeated cultural imperative to work as hard as you possibly can. Hard work, even when it is for a distant and unknown corporate master, has the air of virtue. Further, once we achieve a personal best (the most e-mails sent in an hour, the greatest daily sales of pipe fittings, the most burgers flipped), we are to regard this as nothing more than a mark to be surpassed. In the almost meaningless lexicon of modern management, we are to give 100 percent to our work. Unsatisfied by even that mark, mathematically challenged supervisors sometimes request 110 percent.

Ask what "giving 110 percent" actually means, and you will quickly discover that the idea is not intended to be parsed, defined, or questioned. "It's just something we *say*, for goodness' sake. It doesn't really mean anything." But it keeps getting said.

You are to pour everything into your work: all of your time, your energy, your creativity. You are to leave nothing behind, so you leave at the end of the day an empty shell, like a plastic water bottle or a hot dog wrapper. You are to save nothing for the rest of your life—your spouse, family, friends, interests, health. By starving the sustaining elements of your life, they will drop away, leaving you with only your work to prop you up. But work will never do this, so misery will soon follow.

You should also calculate your capacity for work using an extremely short time horizon. Ask yourself, "How hard can I manage to work today?" Avoid the longer-term questions, like "How hard can I reasonably and sustainably work for a year—or for many years?" The answers to these two queries usually sit in opposition to one another. You can easily work fourteen hours today without burning out or irrevocably damaging your relationships or health, but you cannot work this way forever. For maximum misery, treat the marathon of your work life as though it was a sprint.

The question you must avoid asking is "What is all this work *for*?" In the cave person's era, the answer was obvious. The function of the work was to feed the people doing it. Work was subservient to the demands of life. In the confusion of modern culture, we have succeeded in turning this idea on its head. It is now the function of the person to serve the work and to do so with as small an expectation of reward as possible. The economy is not an instrument for the enhancement of human welfare. Human welfare is an instrument for the enhancement of the economy.

None of this is intended to imply that work has no rewards or has no meaning in itself. Many find fulfillment by striving mightily to excel in their roles—seeing in the completion of a condominium project the creation of homes, in the sale of insurance policies the prevention of financial disaster, in the provision of health care the enhancement of lives. But in these cases, people view the work as their *own* goal, rather than seeing themselves merely as tools for completing the goals of others. To enhance misery, you should instead see yourself as a mere hammer in the hands of the real builder—your boss, the business owner, or the faceless shareholders. Or as the nail being hammered.

Work life can, then, be an effective mechanism for the creation of unhappiness—particularly if one relies on it exclusively to sustain one's life. A one-legged coffee table is dangerously unstable. If dangerous instability is one's goal, then pouring all one's resources and spending all one's time on a single element of existence is an excellent strategy.

LESSON 9

Be Well Informed

It can be challenging to maintain a truly negative point of view in light of the intrusion of sunny days, welcoming friends, buses that occasionally run on time, and savory bagels. The task may prove to be more than you can manage.

What if you had help? What if you could recruit a staff of thousands to scour the globe searching for every negative, misery-inducing thing that happens? They could record these events, photograph them, and then replay them before your eyes.

Well, you're in luck. You *do* have such a staff. The news media will work tirelessly on your behalf to find and report on every disaster, every capsized refugee boat, every failed bridge, every detonated bomb. Television news will then play these accounts for you over and over again, often while you are attempting to eat dinner. You can see bodies, mangled cars, environmental devastation, victims of war, and the squirm-inducing spectacle of reporters rushing the bereaved to ask them how it feels to have terrible things happen to their loved ones.

This downward avenue has been paved and widened in recent decades with the establishment of twenty-four-hour news channels and Internet feeds. In the 1960s (an era of assassinations, the Vietnam war, the tensions between East and West, and massive cultural change) the viewing public had to make do with an hour of televised news once a day. Today we can view tragedy continuously and enjoy the excitement of watching catastrophe unfold in real time.

For this strategy to work, you must avoid certain thoughts (listed below). Fortunately, the media themselves will assist you in your efforts to suppress them.

First, you must not ask yourself why it is so important to learn about tragedies (coups, distant earthquakes, celebrity firings, election results) the moment they occur. The fact that such reports provide you no useful information will only undermine your commitment to viewing. Instead, retain a firm belief in the importance and relevance of "breaking news" and being up to the minute.

Second, you must not ask about the actual information content of the stories presented. They must be seen as worthy in their own right, not because they actually tell you anything. Repetition should be tolerated without complaint, and the lack of detail or balanced analysis must be ignored. You *should* know about the latest bombing in the Middle East, you *should* see the bloodied clothing of the victims, and you *should* attend the funerals by video proxy. Avoid questioning whether this helps any of the people affected.

Third, you should disregard the fact that the content is heavily filtered, seeing it instead as a dispassionate account of the present state of the world. Pay attention only to the coverage of the Pakistani bus that crashed into a gorge, killing twenty-two. Ignore the absence of any mention of the fifty thousand buses that reached their destinations without incident. Regard the scandal of a cabinet minister's expenditures on overpriced orange juice (a recent Canadian news sensation—a tempest in a tumbler) as a complete and sufficient commentary on the judgment and worth of the individual, thus justifying your outrage. Do not withhold your verdict pending additional insight into the person's record or actions.

Finally, the similarities between modern television news and reality television programming should not occur to you, nor should the possibility that much of the news is simply tragedy as entertainment. Perhaps you do not gain anything from the forty-third viewing of the latest shooting, but maybe others will. Yes, it can be disconcerting that coverage of this afternoon's fatal tornado instantly has its own graphics and theme music, but please avoid referring to it as "The Twister Show."

Instead, focus on the value and importance of being well informed. In order to cast a well-considered ballot, in order to decide whether to take the interstate to work, in order to remember to restock the earthquake supplies, in order to decide where to donate money or invest, you need to know these things. The fact that you can learn about all of them more effectively by other means (a quick check of the highway updates, a weekly news magazine that provides more detail with less sensation) must be suppressed.

Cultivate your sympathy for the poor news anchors. For all the tragedy on the planet, they are often left grasping for new information, playing the same footage over and over, interviewing people who were barely affected by events, and scrambling desperately to fill the hours of empty airtime until the next exciting catastrophe.

So monitor your news consumption for a week. Make a note of all your regularly used sources: newsprint, Internet news, radio, late-night news summaries. Televised news at the gym, bank, elevator, subway, or at home. Total it all up. Then strive to increase your exposure next week.

If your attention threatens to wane, play a game. Take two stopwatches and record the number of minutes devoted to events that actually *have* happened versus the consideration of unpleasant events that *might* (or might not) happen at some point in the future. In the absence of real information, the media spend ever-greater proportions of on-air time speculating about potential future events:

- the likelihood of an Ebola outbreak in your country

- possible legislation to be proposed in the current session

- whether a prominent murder trial will invoke an insanity defense

- the possible consequences of another Argentinian debt default

- predicted local traffic patterns for the latter part of the century

Remind yourself that you too will exist in the future, and so it is vital that you have the news even before it has happened—including the news that will never happen at all.

LESSON 10

Set VAPID Goals

One of the best ways to be miserable is to relinquish your goals altogether, thus becoming utterly directionless. But if, like many people, misery is not your *only* goal, then you can dissatisfy yourself with the way you approach your various missions.

Goal setting involves the creation of two categories of ambition. Ultimate goals are the end points of the process: learning Spanish, having a tidy garage, settling on a career, completing a school program, creating a social network, bench pressing two hundred pounds. Ask people about their own goals, and virtually everything they say will be an ultimate goal.

Immediate goals are the small steps in service to an ultimate goal. So if your ultimate goal is to complete your income tax form, then spending twenty minutes gathering the paperwork might be your first immediate goal. If the ultimate goal is to move to Scranton, an immediate goal might be to visit a real estate website for that city.

The cause of misery is well served by failure. So it's important to ignore the so-called SMART rules, which dictate that effective immediate goals should be:

- Specific. You know how you will accomplish the task. "Take the number 19 bus to the Aquatic Center."

- Measurable. You will know whether or not you have succeeded. "Get in pool and swim one lap."

- Action-oriented. Your goal is to do something, not to think or feel a particular way. "Swim the lap— even if I hate it and think my bathing cap looks stupid."

- Realistic. You already know you can do it, even if you don't feel particularly well. "I could swim twenty laps not long ago; I'm absolutely certain I can swim at least one."

- Time-defined. You have a clear time frame for completion of the goal within the coming week. "On Thursday evening."

These rules make success more likely, resulting in increased motivation and interest in the succeeding steps. This only means that you will be more likely to get up off that comfortable couch and continue working on your project. Instead, make all of your immediate goals VAPID:

- Vague. You should be unclear how you are going to complete the goal. If you want to cross-country ski, you should forget all about looking into lessons, thinking about how to get there, or ensuring you have the right clothing.

- Amorphous. The finish line for your immediate goal should be indistinct, so your depressive self can disqualify any progress you have made. Setting a goal to "work on the back garden," for example, allows you to criticize yourself for not finishing everything, thus eliminating any of the satisfaction you might otherwise feel.

- Pie in the sky. Indulge your innate ability to overestimate what you can do. Say that today you will paint the entire house or revamp your company's finances. With the ensuing failure, you will be able to beat yourself up about your incompetence.

- Irrelevant. Tell yourself that if you achieve your ultimate goal of overcoming social anxiety, you will once again be able to visit your bank. You should therefore lock yourself at home studying investment strategy as a "necessary" prerequisite.

- Delayed. Avoid setting a specific time for the completion of your goal. Instead, resolve to get to work the moment you "feel like it." Because it is vanishingly unlikely that you will ever feel like re-caulking the bathroom tile, you can ensure that it will never be done.

Regardless of whether you set SMART or VAPID immediate goals, you can ensure disappointment by—as usual—the simple expedient of following the injunctions of the culture. In this case, keeping your eye on the ball.

Set your ultimate goal (say, to find a long-term relationship), break it down into smaller steps (join the rowing club, accept the invitation to the departmental party, purchase non-droopy underwear), and then, no matter what happens with those immediate goals, continue to hold your attention relentlessly on the ultimate goal. *Am I married yet?*

Most ultimate goals are a long way off—hence the need to break them down into smaller steps. You might achieve them only once, and only after a great deal of effort. If you allow yourself to focus on the immediate goals, you will frequently find that you have succeeded. *Hey, look—I actually smiled at the cute barista.* This runs the risk of increasing your enthusiasm for the path you have created for yourself.

Instead, by stubbornly attending to the ultimate goal (*Have I got a partner yet?*), the discouraging answer (*Well, no*) will recur again and again and again. If there are fifty steps in the process, you will get forty-nine identical answers of "not yet." You can maintain the aura of failure for almost the entire journey. And because this continual discouragement will degrade your interest and motivation, you are likely to give up long before you reach the success of your ultimate goal, thus making the sense of failure permanent.

PART TWO

How to Think Like an Unhappy Person

I am more and more convinced that our happiness or our unhappiness depends far more on the way we meet the events of life than on the nature of those events themselves.

—Wilhelm von Humboldt

Men are disturbed not by things, but by the view which they take of them.

—Epictetus

It's easy to imagine that our emotions—including misery—are produced by the circumstances in which we find ourselves. The phone rings, and we feel anxious. The bills drop through the mail slot, and we feel discouraged.

If we failed to notice the phone or the mail, however, we would not have either of these reactions. Although we cultivate a convincing illusion of the real world, we really have only a passing familiarity with it. Our emotions and our behavior depend not on the events of our lives, but on our perception and evaluation of those events.

We do not stand on a hilltop with an unobstructed view of the real world. Instead, we spend our entire lives within an inner cinema—one with multiple screens lining the walls. One screen shows a series of historical dramas reminiscing about our own past. Another displays speculative fiction about our imagined future. A third shows a documentary of the present moment as it passes just beyond the confines of the theater—a feed of the input from our senses. A fourth sensationalizes and fictionalizes that feed, making wild interpretations of the events it portrays.

The straight documentary is usually the least exciting film on offer. It shows the contours of the furniture around us, the pattern of dust motes in a sunbeam, the sounds of traffic outside, the voices of others, the slow shift of leaves in a breeze, the movement of our hands as we complete a simple task. It is distinguished not by its drama, but by the fact that it portrays the only moment that actually exists: the present one. It is the only non-fiction feature in the cinema.

Because the documentary is less eventful than the other films, we constantly find ourselves distracted by the alternatives. We watch the heavily colorized interpretation screen (*That man walking past right now—he hates you!*), or a humiliating blooper reel from our past (*Remember the time you fell on your face at your sister's wedding?*), or a horror film about the future (*I'm sorry, but the tests reveal you have only a month to live—and by the way, you've been fired*). Our time spent in the pure present is measured in snippets and moments. At times, we find the other screens so distracting that the pure sensory feed seems not to exist at all.

Even when we pay attention to the present, we watch only a tiny portion of the screen. At every moment we receive a vast amount of sensory information, but we process only a fraction of it. For example, notice the sensations of your right foot. Really. Right now. These sensations were available to you before you read that suggestion, but in all probability, you were not focused on them. We react only to the bits of perceptible reality to which we pay attention. Your spouse just thanked you for taking the car in for an oil change—but you don't experience the appreciation unless you pay attention and register that it has been offered.

Further, we slide automatically into interpretation. Ahead of you in the line at the bank, a disheveled man is reaching into his coat pocket. Is he going for his wallet or a gun? Your boss frowns;

is she displeased with your monthly report, or did she overeat at lunchtime? The emotions you feel depend on the interpretations you make.

Misery often develops as a result of the screens we choose to watch in the cranial multiplex—and the films we load into the projectors. We are often such adept projectionists that we do not realize we have selected one storyline over the others, and we mistake the stories for objective reality.

In this section, we examine some of the ways we can deliberately manipulate the mind to produce unhappiness. By carefully choosing the targets of our attention and maximizing the negative evaluations we make, we can turn any summery day into a winter of discontent.

LESSON 11

Rehearse the Regrettable Past

The very fact that you are reading these words suggests that you were not born yesterday. You have a vast storehouse of memories, good and bad, ranging back to early childhood. Whether we do so deliberately or not, a part of everyone's life is spent poking around in the archives and viewing old memories.

Let's begin the process of darkening the mind by sitting back with our popcorn and watching the movie screen of the past. The emotional brain won't know the difference—it reacts whether we are looking at the past, present, or future, and it has a hard time distinguishing between them.

The question, of course, is which reels we should load into the projector. Some elements of almost everyone's past are quite good, some are unpleasant, and many more are quite neutral in tone. In order to increase your misery, you must be selective about the bits of memory you play back to yourself.

The simplest strategy is to focus on the negative, replaying your distressing clips over and over again. Inventory your losses. Remember past injuries. Recall the times you have felt bereft, alone, alienated, terrified, and despondent. Include examples of random, uncontrollable fate knocking you about like a helpless pinball.

Often the most potent clips are those involving personal humiliation:

- the time you wet yourself at elementary school

- the person you thought was a friend who ridiculed you in front of others

- the moment you lost all track of what you were saying while giving a presentation

- your dogged love for a person who clearly had no interest in you

- the job interview you hopelessly failed

- the joke you told at dinner that offended everyone

- the partner who laughed at you in bed

The more you play these, the brighter and more vivid they get and the stronger their link to your gut becomes.

Don't leave them as simple, unconnected memories. Create a narrative of your life to make sense of them. Group them into themes and write a story. Most people easily have enough material for a full-length feature along the lines of: "I am incompetent; my biography is a history of mistakes." Or "No matter how hard I try, eventually everyone abandons me." Or "Catastrophe comes without warning, and I lie helpless in its path."

None of these stories is entirely fictional. Let's face it: you really are incompetent at many things. People really have abandoned you. Uncontrollable things really have happened. Reassure yourself that you are not making these stories up. You have the receipts, photo albums, and scars to prove them.

The fact that you remain standing despite all of these unwelcome events must be ignored. You must not take your history of adversity as a tale of survival or resilience, but as one of defeat. Snuff any hint of pride at what you have lived through. Dwell instead on the damage—the *irreparable* damage—that these events have wrought upon your person and your psyche.

To strengthen the narrative, ensure that you focus on events that prove your thesis. Neglect the fact that, despite failing calculus, you are good at car repair. Forget that, despite the distracted absence of your father, you had an aunt who doted upon you. Highlight the car accident that injured you, and leave unrehearsed the memory of the birth of your child.

You need not flush away all of your positive memories, however. Dante suggested, "There is no greater sorrow than recalling your happy days in a time of misery."[5] You can use positive memories to contrast the golden past with the drab present. Dwell on how wonderful that old bohemian apartment of yours was—or that relationship, that job, that city, that sparkling, halcyon time in your life—and remind yourself that it is now over. You have lost it forever. Ignore any positive aspects of your current life—your nicer home, your improved bank balance, the knowledge that you did, in fact, survive past thirty—that were absent in the romanticized past.

You can also disqualify and thereby erase your good memories:

- You have fond recollections of your first love, but with the darkness of hindsight, you can see that it was always doomed and that what you thought was love was really a delusion on your part.

- You truly enjoyed rock climbing in your twenties, but now you realize what idiots you and your friends were and how close you came to disaster.

- You got that award at work a few years ago, but it's now clear they were just setting you up to take on a futile project that has since made your life hell.

What you thought was happiness was a mistake. Your misery has, all along, been the truth.

Ensure that you do not engage in this reinterpretation process with negative memories. We often discover that events that seemed awful at the time were necessary in order for positive developments that followed. The breakup of that relationship tore your heart out, but you now know that it would never have worked anyway and that you needed to be single to meet, the following year, the person you have been with ever since. Your cycling injury was severe and painful, but without it, you would never have found your calling in the field of traffic safety. Realizing that the disappointments and disasters of the past were necessary for you to be the person you are today serves only to lessen their sting. You want the venom to be as potent as possible.

Blame Inward, Give Credit Outward

Dan Savage, the brutally direct sex advice columnist, is fond of skewering correspondents who describe a long and predictably disastrous series of events and then disavow all personal responsibility for the outcome. "So you put that object where it was never meant to go," he might observe, "and you lost it and had to go to the emergency room." Then he follows it up with one of his signature phrases. "HTH?" he asks. "How'd that happen?"

We might ask the same thing about the events of our own lives. We get a letter from the government informing us that our tax return was incorrect and that we owe them another $1,252. This isn't a random event; something brought it about. So, HTH? How'd that happen?

Renowned psychologist Martin Seligman focused for much of his career on the sources of lowered mood. He and his colleagues studied people's ideas about the causes of different types of events and categorized their attributions:

- *Internal or external.* An internal attribution attributes the primary cause to oneself: *I was the one who made the mistake on the tax form.* An external attribution emphasizes other factors: *The government deliberately makes these forms hard to understand.*

- *Global or specific.* The attribution might generalize beyond the situation at hand (*The government never cares about the people who have to fill in its forms*) or could stay with the individual event (*Whoever wrote that line of the tax guide wasn't thinking clearly*).

- *Stable or unstable.* A stable cause is unlikely to change over time: *I'm an idiot at filling in these forms—always have been.* An unstable one is more situational and so less likely to recur: *I was stressed out when I did my taxes because the parakeet was sick.*

Happy people tend to show a degree of balance in their attributional style. For example, an employee might receive the annual review of her work. Good or bad, she will likely attribute the details to a mix of her own performance (*They're right. I did work hard this year, and I did make that mistake on the Smith account*) and externally to the job or the evaluator (*Joan helped me a lot on the Chan file, so I can't take all the credit, and the lease foul-up was partly the property manager's fault*). Some evidence suggests that particularly happy people tend to look a bit more on the bright side than might really be merited, blaming circumstance for bad outcomes and magnifying their own role in positive ones.

The bias seems to be stronger (and flipped to the negative), however, in the depressed. The attributions made by people in deepest misery tend to depend very much on whether the event is positive or negative. Positive events, like getting a promotion, scoring well on a test, or learning to water-ski, most often receive external attributions. The miserable will say that the task was just easy or that they were lucky. "Anyone could have passed that test," they say. "Water-skiing is stupidly simple."

In other words, the positive outcome has nothing to do with them. Although they might get a mild lift from the event, they do not interpret any deeper meaning from it in terms of their abilities or talents. The attributions for welcome events tend to be external (*This says nothing about me*), specific (*Water-skiing is the only thing I do right*), and unstable over time (*Next time I'll probably break a leg*).

Negative events, on the other hand, tend to be given attributions that are internal, global, and stable. A fender bender in the supermarket parking lot, for example: *I'm a bad driver. Always have been.* Getting dumped by a partner: *When people get to know me, they don't want me. I'm unlovable.* Rain during a beach picnic: *I have never been able to plan things properly; everything I do gets ruined.* These unwelcome events are viewed as being all about the person.

Needless to say, this is a game anyone can play. First, check out your existing style:

- Think of three positive and three negative events that have happened in the past month. Write them down.

- For each, ask the Dan Savage question: HTH? How'd that happen? Write down the first explanation that comes to mind.

Then take a look at your attributions. Internal or external? Global or specific? Stable or unstable? You're looking for a pattern that separates the positives from the negatives. Misery is best induced with external-specific-unstable for positives and internal-global-stable for negatives.

If you show the expected pattern, congratulations! You have already mastered this technique. Keep up the good work. You may skip merrily ahead to the next lesson.

If you don't show this pattern, congratulations again! You have just discovered a new and unexplored avenue into the valley of unhappiness. Go back over your situations and rework your attributions. If something good (like passing your driver's exam) happened, notice how it might be the product of luck, the undeserved generosity of others, or the ease of the task involved. Downplay your own role. *That examiner was napping. He didn't notice that I hit the curb when I parallel parked.*

For your unwelcome situations (like a car breakdown), make it all about you—your stupidity, incompetence, or unlovability. *I didn't get the oil changed even though I knew it was due. Careless, clueless, and doomed—that's me.*

Once you've reworked your situations on paper, look out for new events—positive and negative. Work at practicing a slanted attributional style with them as they occur. When you have mastered this strategy, you should be able to drain the uplift of any positive event and maximize the impact of any negative one.

Practice the "Three Bad Things" Exercise

Martin Seligman, mentioned in the preceding lesson, is a traitor to our cause. Unsatisfied with working exclusively on what we might call "negative psychology," he abandoned ship in the 1990s and began to study the determinants of better-than-average well-being. Happy people inhabit a state that has been, at least until lately, psychology's "undiscovered country."

Rather than simply enumerating the correlates of high life satisfaction, Seligman and his colleagues have devised exercises to boost it. This new field of positive psychology might seem to have little to teach us about misery. But just as risk factors for depression can point the way toward happiness, satisfaction-enhancing techniques can inform us of what might bring despair.

One of the most potent strategies thus far studied is also an arrestingly simple one. Lying in bed, before going to sleep, you would call to mind three things about the day that you enjoyed or appreciated. These events can be worldly—perhaps, for example, a peace treaty appeared in the news or a friend received a promotion. But most of the events should be personal: a tasty bagel eaten at breakfast, a compliment received from a friend, a bookshelf newly dusted, a drive through morning rush hour that was easier than usual. Even on an otherwise terrible day, there are usually at least some positive elements: *The admitting clerk at the root canal clinic smiled nicely at me.*

To get people to remain focused a bit longer on the exercise, Seligman advises them to write the events down in a bedside notebook and to contemplate how they came about—in effect, to make attributions for the events. They might credit the bagel to the skill of the baker, the compliment to a friend's kindness, the clean bookshelf to their own efforts, the light traffic to people taking a long weekend. Some of these attributions might be internal, others external. The point is to occupy the mind with these positive events for at least a few minutes.

The challenge that clinicians have in recommending this exercise is that it seems far too simple. People want to believe that changing how they feel is a complex, obstacle-strewn path filled with thorns and leg-hold traps. It turns out, however, that altering the mood is often a somewhat simpler task, both for those seeking happiness and for those of us with darker aspirations.

How does the exercise work in the quest for increased misery? As we have been discussing, the key to negativity is to set our cognitive filter so it weeds out positive events and emphasizes the unpleasant ones. The Three Things exercise pushes the filter the other way, forcing one to pay attention, however briefly, to the more welcome elements of life. Once people are accustomed to the nighttime exercise, they can, without prompting, begin doing the same thing throughout the day, in effect noticing and storing up material for their bedtime ritual. *I should remember getting this check in the mail; I can use it as one of my three things tonight.*

All right, but we're driving in the wrong direction, aren't we? The corresponding exercise for our purposes is obvious. Each evening, as you settle into bed, cast your mind back over the day. Think of three things that brought your mood lower. Even seemingly pleasant days will have a few:

- I tripped getting onto the bus and made a fool of myself.

- My tea spilled on my computer keyboard and probably ruined it.

- I stepped in the dog poop I was trying to scoop up—while wearing my open-toes.

Anything will do—no need to find the worst. Hold each in your mind for a few seconds. Dwell on why they occurred. Extra points if you can blame yourself. Write them down. Then let them go. Pledge to carry out the exercise for at least a week.

Of course, doing this will likely trigger rumination and keep you awake, thus achieving a spinoff effect that positive psychologists can only dream about. And, like the happiness collectors, you will automatically accentuate your daytime habit of looking for bedtime candidates (in your case, negative ones) as they occur.

For extra impact, install a turbocharger on the technique. Once you have listed your daily three disappointments, cast your mind forward to the day to come. List three unpleasant things that *might* happen:

- My boss will probably demand that report I haven't yet completed.

- I have to return the phone call from the city's zoning department, which won't be good.

- In the evening we have dinner scheduled with my alcoholic father-in-law.

Think about each in turn, then roll over and slide gently off to sleep.

Good luck with that.

LESSON 14

Construct Future Hells

In an episode of the old program *The Twilight Zone*, a man awakens in his home and cannot open his dresser drawer. It emerges that he has accidentally voyaged too far forward in time. He learns that every minute of every day is constructed separately by a team of carpenters and that the particular minute he finds himself in is not yet ready for occupancy.

This sounds far-fetched, but it is precisely what we do with the imaginary land in which we spend much of every waking day: the future. We make it up. We cannot be certain that an undetected asteroid won't strike in the night, obliterating our—or everyone's—future entirely. Every vision of the future we have is just a fantasy.

You do not own a crystal ball. The future is always uncertain. It will probably be a mixed bag of good and bad, but most of your feared catastrophes will never happen. Many of us are uncomfortably aware that we spend an inordinate amount of mental effort imagining disasters that are extremely unlikely (the firing, the terminal diagnosis, the bankruptcy), and almost no time contemplating the more probable outcomes (going to work next week having not been fired, being told the blood tests are fine, getting through the financial squeeze). This is a perfect path to misery. To get there, you should believe wholeheartedly the anxiety-ridden horror films you play on the screen of your future.

There's an added treat to the fact that the future is uncertain. Whereas each of us has only a single past, the future has the advantage of multiplicity: we can create endless variations. Consider the possible outcomes of an upcoming business trip, the likelihood of each outcome, and the amount of time you might spend thinking of them:

- The plane to Chicago crashes (vanishingly unlikely; two hours of thought).

- You discover you haven't packed something essential, like pants (unlikely, and anyway, Chicago has stores; thirty minutes of thought).

- You blank out in the middle of the presentation, panic, and begin to cry (never happened yet; seven hours of thought).

- Everything goes fine (the most likely outcome; zero minutes of thought).

We can do this for everything in our lives. We can worry both about not getting the job we just interviewed for and about getting it and failing in the role. We can create situations with ten different resolutions, all bad, and we can feel the pain of all of them. We can be rejected by potential partners a thousand times without ever making an approach.

Try it. Think of something negative that could conceivably happen in coming weeks (or perhaps an item from your "Three Bad Things" exercise) and about which you have been worrying. Turn that thought into a miniature drama, a made-for-me movie, with color and surround sound:

- Your idea for a guidebook to misery is declined. See the rejection letter come through the slot and envision the expression on the face of the scornful and overworked submissions editor.

Now here's the tricky part. You know that this image is a possibility, not a fact. It has a certain likelihood of occurring, which means it has a corresponding likelihood that it won't. See if you can shift it from something that *might* happen to something that surely *will*. Then plug in the emotions and react to the knowledge that this is your path. The track has been laid, and this is where it goes. Then construct a chain of events, turning your brief scenario into the first act of a movie:

- Discouraged, you give up on writing and resolve, henceforth, to take up drinking instead.

This moment, too, is a choice point of multiple possibilities. Select the worst and create a new film of that outcome:

- You become dependent on alcohol, ruining all of your relationships, and are abandoned by everyone.

Continue on, laying each piece of track downhill, section by section:

- Too dysfunctional and hostile to work at paid employment, you lose your home and are cast out onto the street.

- The local newspaper selects you as an example of self-induced destruction and presses for the elimination of all societal safety nets nationwide.

- Angered by the loss of their supports and treatment programs, a torch-bearing army of your fellows descends upon the alley in which you live, and sets your cardboard box alight—the one on which you have written the potential bestseller documenting your decline.

- Feel the impact as you watch your words go up in flames.

You may find that at some point your catastrophizing begins to lose its grip on your emotions, just as stamping on an accelerator pedal while stuck in snow may cause the wheels to spin. It becomes difficult to make yourself feel the magnitude of the disaster. No problem. Simply wind it back a few steps to the point just before plausibility was lost. Play and replay the movie to that moment:

- the gasps as you enter the conference room pantsless

- the flickering lights of the ambulance

- the disappointment in your children's eyes as you are led away by police

People often wonder how the very fortunate can ever be miserable. They have wealth, health, partners, family, and friends. What's not to like? As often as not, this strategy is key to their feelings. The higher the rollercoaster goes, the longer the coming drop can be. The better your life is, the more miserable you can make yourself by the contemplation of losing it all.

LESSON 15

Value Hope Over Action

We have discussed how the future extends before us along a diverging set of pathways, a peacock's tail of possibility. Every moment brings us to another fork in the road. On most days, we don't have earth-shattering decisions to make, such as "Shall I emigrate?" or "Should I call off the wedding?" But every decision we make, big or small, selects a branch to a different future. We stand before a dizzying array of nameless doors, and every time we open one, we find ourselves with another set of choices to make.

Given that our emotions are based largely on our thoughts, one way to feel worse is to use the strategy described in the preceding lesson: focus on the potential disasters. Another is more subtle: seize upon and hope for one of the rosier options.

This might seem odd. Won't hope for a shining future backfire and produce happiness instead? This, after all, is why most people are so drawn to hope. Yes, the contemplation of tomorrow's wonders may well make us cheerful—for a time. Our old friend misery, however, lurks just around the corner.

The challenge is that although we can imagine various futures, we cannot guarantee they will come about. No matter how hard we hope for Future A, we cannot eliminate the chance that Futures X, Y, or Z will transpire instead. We might guess that our odds of scoring tickets to the Iron Maiden concert are 65 percent, but this only prompts our brain to remind us of the 35 percent chance of disappointment.

Hope, then, is always a two-sided coin. You might get the outcome you wanted, but then again, you might not. This is why Buddhists often speak of hope as a combination package: hope-and-fear. Hope summons fear as a natural accompaniment, like Batman and Robin, ham and cheese, or smoke and fire. You seldom get one without the other. Pinning your present happiness on a bright but conditional future automatically sows the seeds of misery-inducing anxiety:

- It would be so wonderful if…

- Oh, but what if…

When you attempt to brighten your mood with visions of the job you just applied for, you become uncomfortably aware that you may not get it. The joy of hope, then, is as brittle as the skin on a crème brûlée. You can feel yourself sliding out over thin ice, conscious of the depths beneath.

Further, both hope and fear come from a focus on the imaginary future rather than the singular moment of present reality. It is in the present that we actually live, in the present that we have a degree of real influence, and in the present that our misery can be most easily interrupted by contentment, satisfaction, and calm. The present is almost always manageable, though it is typically less exciting than the melodramas playing out on the other screens of the mental cinema—hence the difficulty that aficionados of mindfulness report in keeping their minds there. Misery is easier.

Ah, but what if hope is used to guide our behavior? What if we create a vision of the future, then lay out the steps to get there and set out on the journey? This is perhaps the only way that a focus on hope may defeat our quest for discontent. Even here, however, hope brings along its anxious twin. We might do all we can to secure the job we have envisioned, but still we cannot stamp out the possibility that they will find someone who is better qualified.

It is more useful, however, simply to use hope as a substitute for action, which is what we usually do anyway. We entertain ourselves with lovely visions but do nothing to make them materialize. Nowhere is this phenomenon more evident than in the assertions of *The Secret*, a book and film created by an Australian reality-television producer. Advocates of the "Law of Attraction" believe that carefully envisioning specific outcomes actually causes the lines of the future to shift, bringing objectives closer. Imagine a future spouse, for example, and one may come knocking at the door.

It's easy to see how this principle might actually work, if it causes subtle shifts in our behavior. By envisioning a partner, perhaps we will get out more, take better care of ourselves, and smile more frequently in the direction of members of our preferred gender. All of these changes could work to increase the odds of partnership. The "Secret" is not supposed to operate via our own efforts, however, but through mysterious forces in the universe.

A belief that "hoping will make it so" is an ideal example of the usefulness of hope in the promotion of misery—particularly given that it is so demonstrably false. Witness the millions who purchase lottery tickets, entertaining clear visions of winning but failing to do so; the candidates anticipating election and being defeated at the polls; the entrepreneurs whose businesses fail—and the rancorous lawsuits over the profits of *The Secret* itself. A belief in the power of pure hope over action pulls us from contact with our actual present-day lives, promotes anxiety, and encourages a passive and ineffective approach to the realization of our goals.

So go ahead. Hope. Try to boost your mood by fixating on an imagined future. Long for your fantasy to come true. Your anxiety will build, your efforts will cease, and your present will pass unnoticed. Perfect for creating unhappiness.

Become a Toxic Optimist

What's this, a rerun? How is optimism separate from hope? They both involve an emphasis on positive futures, but whereas hope involves pining for a positive outcome, toxic optimism counts on it. It seduces us into stepping, like the protagonist of Voltaire's *Candide*, toward a rosy future that exists only in our own minds.

Optimism seems like such a positive idea, and indeed, many optimists seem far from miserable—particularly when they describe the glowing future that awaits them. But by neglecting the potential pitfalls, they set out on the road to misery.

Consider an example. A distant acquaintance developed a business idea that made him extremely excited. It was brilliant, it was simple, and it was obvious to him that it would work. Wanting to safeguard the plan and surround himself only with positive energy, he kept the product secret while expounding on the plans he was making. He invested all he had in the enterprise. When he finally revealed the concept—a personalized ball-cap business—those closest to him looked at one another in surprise. This was the big idea? Few thought it would fly, but he would hear none of it—besides, the investment had already been made. Sure enough, within two years he lost everything. Optimism in toxic excess is bad for business.

There are three critical features of toxic optimism that you will want to harness.

Probability Inflation. Manipulate the odds, inflating the likelihood that the desired outcome will come to pass. You want it, so assume it's going to happen:

- You want the job, so you believe you'll get it.

- You want to get across town in thirty minutes, so you're confident traffic will be light.

- You want the citizens of the country we bomb to welcome us, so it seems inevitable that they will.

Hide from yourself the fact that you have stacked the deck. Make sure that it seems that you are looking at the situation clearly and without bias. Actually, of course, your desires have colored the lens. As you look ahead, you want to see only a wide, straight, yellow-brick road leading directly to the Emerald City; no disgruntled sister-witches or winged monkeys lining the route. When you tell dispassionate observers about your projections, they may shake their heads, unswayed by your enthusiasm. But since you are certain that they just don't have your level of insight, you can ignore their cautions and overcommit to an unwise course of action.

Selective Attention. Focus all of your attention on the course you desire and ignore the courses you don't. Toss contingency planning out the window:

- Why come up with other products? Your $50 ball caps are a guaranteed hit.

- Why take a lifejacket? The boat isn't going to tip over.

- Why pack a coat? It's sure to be sunny in the mountains.

- Why use a condom? This person looks perfectly healthy.

Once you have mastered this skill, unpleasant possibilities may not occur to you at all. Insurance? Why would you need that?

Elevated Expectations. A third aspect of toxic optimism is that, having assumed the future will work out as anticipated, your vision can become the baseline for your emotions. Knowing that you will get the promotion, you incorporate this into the plan of your life. Should the promotion actually come your way, you will get no great lift, because you were counting on it anyway. Should the position be handed to someone else, however, then the great yawning maw of an unforgiving and incomprehensible universe will stare you in the face. Because you have already spent the anticipated raise, you will face poverty.

Most of our dreams do not come to pass. Consequently, toxic optimism will encase you in a near-constant state of disappointment—a world in which the shining future is never quite matched by the drab present. Eventually it will become more and more difficult to sustain yourself with visions of tomorrow's sugarplums when all you seem to receive are dry and tasteless prunes.

Full disclosure: although I am quite good at many of the strategies in this book, this one is beyond my skill level. I was raised by pessimists. "You just wait" was the motto of my childhood. Every plane will crash. Every train will derail. Every automobile will run out of gas. This way of thinking became so wedged in my unconscious that I am incapable of doing without Plans B, C, and D. Left to my own devices, I would wear a lifejacket in a desert rainshower.

You too will find that some of these strategies simply do not fit with your nature. If you have chosen this book, however, perhaps it is because misery does not seem to be among your native talents. If your outlook is distressingly, perpetually sunny, then this technique, which involves indulging your natural optimism, may well prove one of your most powerful methods of summoning the storm clouds.

Is optimism always a reliable path to misery? Alas, no. There is an alternative form of optimism—perhaps better called *realism*—that instead tends to produce greater contentment and so must be avoided. Like so many paths to happiness, it leads along the middle path, the Goldilocks route.

Realistic optimists acknowledge the full range of potential futures, good and bad, and attempt to get a truly dispassionate sense of the likelihood of each without reference to personal desire. Knowing that their guesses are never perfect, they may consult with others who do not share their attachment to one outcome over the others. "What do you think of this new boyfriend of mine, really?"

Thus informed, they take steps to increase the likelihood of their desired outcomes while cautiously planning contingencies should the negative ones transpire instead. "Plan for the best, prepare for the worst" is their motto. Yours, by contrast, should be "Assume the best, ignore the worst."

LESSON 17

Filter for the Negative

We've been looking for misery in the internal cinema, and so far, we have found it by focusing our attention on the past and future screens. The movie screen of the present also offers strategies for lowering our mood. The first of these involves carefully selecting which parts of the screen to watch and ignoring the rest.

Let's try it out. In your home at this moment, many things are true:

- The carpet in the front hall has a pleasing pattern.

- There is an electricity bill, as yet unpaid, on the sideboard.

- The laundry has mostly been done and put away.

- The bookcase was dusted recently.

- The yogurt you purchased yesterday has already got mold on it.

- The warm sun is coming in through the window.

- The cat has thrown up on your bed.

- You own a microwave oven that can heat food in minutes.

How do you feel?

The human mind is simply not capable of paying attention to everything at once. At best, you can shift your focus from one to another. Even then, you don't give them all equal time. There are some facts that attract your attention frequently (*There's a scary stack of papers on the counter!*) and others that never cross your mind (*The furnace is completely reliable*). If there are good things about your home that you never consider, they will have no real impact on your mood. If, on the other hand, you focus your mind entirely on the unpaid bill, the spotty yogurt, and the cat vomit, they alone will determine your emotional tone.

The human brain developed, in large part, as a problem-solving organ. It has a bias to look for the things that are wrong rather than those that are right. Evolution, then, is clearly on the side of the miserable.

Your emotions are governed not by the circumstances of your life, but by the circumstances to which you pay attention. In order to become more miserable, give in to your natural tendencies, and direct your attention exclusively to the problem areas of your life:

- Think only of the colleague who is annoyed with you, not the others who are impressed.

- Dwell on the part of your job that you still don't understand; ignore the areas you have mastered.

- Preoccupy yourself with your spouse's failings; never list his or her good points.

Friends may occasionally tell you not to worry, saying that there's nothing wrong. You can safely ignore them. You have a multifaceted life. There is *always* something wrong, and there always will be.

It is enough to emphasize the negatives. Don't bother trying to blot out the positives. To do that, you'd have to inventory and acknowledge them, then push them aside. This brings them to mind, if only briefly, which runs the risk that they might momentarily lodge there and lift your spirits. If you find it difficult to focus exclusively on the negative, you can give yourself the odd break by examining the neutral, the ho-hum minutiae of daily existence. *Oh, look, the light is off in the kitchen. It's Tuesday today. The cat's name is Snuggles.*

You can do more. Certain negatives, like cat vomit on your sheets, effortlessly push you in an unhappy direction. Your interpretation practically writes itself. But you can focus on the meaning and significance of the event to maximize the effect.

In cognitive therapy, we often conduct an exercise called the "Downward Arrow" to detect the form of a person's negative thinking. This involves starting with the event and the emotion it evokes, then digging about for the interpretation the person has imposed on it. Once we have the interpretation, we invite the person to assume it is correct. "And what would happen next?" we ask. "And what would the worst thing about that be? And what would that mean?"

You can do this yourself—in fact, to at least some extent, you probably already do. Write down one of your negatives. Then run away with it and marry it in Vegas:

- I'm going to have to launder those sheets again.

- And I don't have time before I leave for work.

- And it'll be late when I get home.

- So I won't get enough sleep.

- And I'll look like an idiot at that department meeting tomorrow.

- And pretty soon they'll fire me.

- I'll never get another job without a reference.

- And I'll have to move back in with my aging parents.

- They have an incontinent dog.

On no account should you strive for balance. *At least the cat got the sheets this time and not my toothbrush. He's done this before; he'll do it again. He's probably fine. And I have a spare set of sheets, so I can clean these later. I'm okay. Now let's get to work.* Instead, you must stick to the negative.

By indulging in your innate tendency to catastrophize, your emotions can be governed not by the already discouraging sight of cat vomit, but by the prospect of slinking back to Mom and Dad. And probably coming home to a dead cat.

Cultivate Your Presence—Elsewhere

Are you reading this in a coffee shop? There are dozens of other coffee shops you might have chosen, other beverages you might have ordered, and other books you might have taken along. If you're not in a coffee shop—well, you might have been.

The situation in which you find yourself is singular. Just as the present moment is the only one that truly exists, given that the past is gone and the future is a fantasy, your current situation is the only real one open to you. The option you chose is the one you have.

The alternatives, however, are always multiple. You could be in the park, at the beach, home in bed, hanging upside-down at the climbing wall. The odds that you made the best selection from the hundreds or thousands of options that were open to you are pretty minimal. The best home, partner, job, city, friends, belt, education, menu item? The best book to be reading right now? Surely one of those other choices would have been at least a little bit better.

You can almost always envision an alternative that might have been preferable to the one you chose. Here's the strategy:

1. Think back to the options that seemed available to you at some earlier time—that smile from the letter carrier, that other book at the shop, the red pants you might have put on this morning, the moment in high school when you chose history over physics.

2. Like a locomotive in a switching yard, back yourself up to the decision point, then take the other path in your mind.

3. Though you don't really know what that option would have been like (perhaps the letter carrier was a pickup artist), imagine your limitless satisfaction on that other path. You would have been so happy, so wealthy, so successful, so loved.

4. Contrast this with the somewhat drab and no-big-deal quality of your actual existence—the mediocre coffee served in this shop, the mediocre love served in your bed. Feel the pain of regret as you play and replay the lost footage of the path not taken.

5. Attack yourself for eschewing a path that was so obviously superior. You are a fool, a dupe, a fashion victim, stupidly impulsive, pathetically cautious, lacking insight, immature, attracted to bright and shiny objects, stuck in a rut.

6. Switch mentally from your role as ruthlessly judgmental critic to penitent recipient and slather a thick layer of shame atop your regret like cream cheese frosting on a carrot cake.

7. Spread the misery by loudly proclaiming your dissatisfaction to anyone nearby. "If I hadn't been so stupid as to marry *you...*"

You can use this strategy wherever you are, no matter how big or small the situation. In a restaurant, you can dwell on the really great meals you had in other establishments. In the multiplex, you can imagine the terrific films playing out on the other screens. While traveling, you can contemplate the charms of the destinations you bypassed for this one. On the road, you can think about the better traffic patterns on other routes. At your desk, you can long for the fun of other jobs you might have taken. At home, you can compare your daughter's love of the drums to the blissful silence from the childless couple's home next door.

Although this prescription may seem simple, there are tricky elements. First, you must disregard any features of your present situation that are superior to the alternatives. Dwell on the better location of the camping area you might have chosen over the one you did. Ignore the fact that the alternative site is presently being pelted with rain.

Second, you must avoid any awareness of alternatives that might have been even worse than the one you chose. True, you turned down a date with the nerdy programmer who subsequently made billions, but you also filtered out several who presently reside in federal custody. Thinking about the roads best not taken, you will only risk feeling pleased with the one you are on.

Third, you must ignore the fact that you really haven't taken those alternatives and that, as a result, your comparison is based entirely on a fantasy. Perhaps, having accepted that job offer in Cincinnati, you would have stepped out of the airport and been hit by a bus. You don't really know. Instead, assume that your vision about how things might have been is flawlessly accurate.

If, for some reason, you are unable or unwilling to blame yourself for the path you are on, all is not lost. Lay the responsibility at someone else's doorstep instead. "Sarojni was the one who told me to buy this lemon of a car." This will fan the flames of angry resentment and damage a friendship, adding to the regret of a disappointing purchase. If no other perpetrators suggest themselves, you can blame the fates (*Everything happens to me!*) and rehearse the sense of being an insignificant leaf tossed about by a hostile and anonymous storm.

Concerned that perhaps you are being unfair to your present experience? Nonsense. There is validity to this grass-is-greener strategy. If you have succeeded in making yourself miserable, those other places really *are* more fun to be—if only because right now you are not there to spoil them.

LESSON 19

Insist on Perfection

So far we have been concerned with our appraisals of the outside world—past, present, or future. But hidden off to one side in the theater of the mind is yet another screen which, upon closer examination, proves to be a mirror. Much of our misery results from the way we view ourselves—particularly in the way we compare our performance against unattainable standards.

Whenever you attempt a task, you automatically create expectations about the outcome:

- Build a doghouse, and you have an image in your mind of how it should look.

- Bake a flan, and you imagine how it will taste.

- Step into a kayak for the first time, and you fanta-size about remaining dry.

The degree of attachment to your envisioned outcome can vary. You might think, *Well, who knows? Let's just try it. Que sera, sera. Whatever will be, will be.* Or you might be firmly determined. *Damn it, I need this presentation to go without a hitch.*

If you are dedicated to the pursuit of misery, strive for perfection. If today you hit a new high-water mark, strive for more tomorrow. Believe that there is no such thing as "good enough" in any area of your life.

This way of thinking defines satisfaction—the emotional state associated with "enough" and "fine as it is"—as unattainable or, if attained, as the result of a delusion. The only way to relax when adopting this frame of mind is to be utterly flawless. Any deficiencies, any sloppiness, any errors are unacceptable.

Cheerful, unworried people (those whose mental state resembles that of a golden retriever) tend to split their expectations in two:

- a minimum level of performance about which they would feel content

- an aspirational level, which they may not seriously expect to reach and to which they do not feel extremely attached

They reveal these twin achievement lines when they talk about their expectations. "I'm just hoping not to fall out of the boat and drown. But it would be fun to find out I'm great at this." "It would be nice to ace this exam, but I'll be happy just to pass it." "I'd love to have *Better Dogs and Hydrants* feature my doghouse on the cover, but it will be enough if it just keeps rain off the dog." Pitching their minimum expectations low, they are almost always relaxed and sanguine about their outcomes.

But this, clearly, is how to feel happier about one's performance. To become more miserable, bring the two lines closer together. If possible, combine them into a single, all-but-impossible high bar over which you will seldom be able to jump. Regard anything less than perfection as humiliating and disastrous, reflecting badly on your worth as a human being. Scorn the idea of an easier bar over which you could certainly hop. Tell yourself that people who hold those kinds of standards are lazy, unambitious slobs who never get anywhere in life. Surely only those for whom nothing is good enough actually achieve anything.

This strategy enables you to feel badly about yourself regardless of your level of actual achievement. If you get 99 percent on the exam, you can torture yourself with the idiocy of the one mistake you made. You may prove stronger and faster than your kayaking instructor, but you can still feel humiliated by her superior form. No matter how good a weight lifter you are, there will always be a tonnage that is beyond you.

As usual, you have to ignore a few inconvenient facts to make this work:

- People who adopt reasonable standards generally achieve as much or more than perfectionists, because they get a motivational boost from success, enabling them to devote more energy to their efforts.

- Perfectionism imposes a fear of trying out new things out of a knowledge that you will not excel on your first try. This results in a restricted life.

- Perfectionism can cause you to spend a lot of time erasing minor flaws that no one else can see, inadvertently annoying people with your slowness and preventing you from shifting to other challenges.

You don't have to be satisfied with disappointing yourself. The highest level of perfectionistic excellence is to imagine that everyone around you expects you to be perfect as well. This way of thinking is called "socially prescribed perfectionism,"[6] and research shows that it is especially effective at leading to misery.

To engage in socially prescribed perfectionism, you could surround yourself with a cohort of the most exacting, judgmental people on the planet. This really isn't necessary, however. Remember that your emotions are based on your *beliefs* about reality, not reality itself. So it's enough just to assume that your friends and family hold these unreasonable standards, whatever their real opinions might be.

In this way, you can feel acutely self-conscious about everything you do and constantly see disgust and scorn in the eyes of others. Whenever you are out in public, you can feel that you are a humiliation and an embarrassment—not only to yourself, but also to your family, friends, and coworkers. When you are alone, you can avoid experiencing relief by telling yourself that it is only a matter of time before you have to sally forth into the outside world again. And then people will find out what you have been doing—and judge you for the unproductive, incompetent failure that you believe yourself to be.

Rely upon your ability to mind-read others. Don't check out their opinions. *No need for them to tell me, I know they wish I were better.*

- Do they really expect your lawn to look like a golf green?

- Do they honestly believe that your every e-mail should win the Pulitzer Prize?

- Do they imagine that you know everything about ancient Greece?

Of course they do. Be suspicious of any statements they make to the contrary. When they reassure you or look happy with your accomplishments, they are simply being polite.

Do not ask yourself whether your perceptions are coming, perhaps, from your own fears or insecurities, rather than from your flawless ability to tell what people are thinking. Suppress considerations of what you expect (or demand) of your peers and why you believe that everyone else expects so much more from you. Avoid wondering whether, if they did hold such unreasonable expectations, it might be best to ignore them anyway. This might weaken your resolve to keep attempting the unattainable.

You don't want to be one of those cheerful golden retrievers, after all. You're trying to build the doghouse, not live in it.

Work Endlessly on Your Self-Esteem

Do you have a cat? If so, does it seem to think well of itself, or does it appear to slink around in deep shame at being an inferior sort of feline?

Most people sense that the cats they know have perfectly high self-esteem—despite never having had psychotherapy, attending no esteem-building workshops, and reading very few self-help books. How do they do it?

We live in a culture with a deep and abiding faith in the concept of self-esteem. To follow this particular path downward, all you have to do is go along with the crowd. Like them, view self-esteem as something that you are born without and must build up, brick by brick, into a tall and sturdy structure. Assume that self-esteem is something separate from confidence in your ability to perform any particular task, like juggling or changing the oil in your car. This makes it vague and amorphous enough that constructing it becomes a futile—and thus misery-inducing—effort.

But wait. Isn't self-esteem real? You've been taught about it since birth. It can't possibly be just another Easter Bunny, can it?

Let's find out. Imagine a person with terrible self-esteem visiting the bank and then walking to a café for lunch. What's he thinking about?

I probably looked like an idiot when I dropped my pen back there, and the teller could see my bank balance— she probably thought I'm a complete failure. Even now, these people on the sidewalk can see what a loser I am, and my hair is sticking up everywhere. When I get lunch, I'll probably spill it on myself and look even worse.

Sound plausible?

Now imagine a person with great self-esteem doing the same thing. What's he thinking about?

Wow, I really impressed them all at the bank back there—when I bent over to pick up my pen they could see how toned my rear end is, after all that work at the gym, and my balance probably made the teller drool. Look at all these lucky people sharing the sidewalk with me, envying me for my great hair. And when I get to the café, they'll put me at the table in the front window to attract other customers. Hey, I know: let me recite positive affirmations to myself on the way.

You think?

Or is he more likely to be wondering, *Do I want the soup or just a chicken sandwich?*

The truth is, people with good self-esteem are not constantly evaluating themselves. It's the ones without it who do this. Our culture teaches us that having self-esteem is an active process of building ourselves up. It isn't. Cats, three-year-olds, and adults with good self-esteem aren't doing much of anything—they're just focused on the task at hand.

The active process is to have *low* self-esteem, to be constantly tearing ourselves down. When we wake up in the morning, before our mind starts going, our self-esteem is fine. We only begin feeling inadequate when we start rehearsing the negative story that we tell ourselves. By focusing on self-esteem, we cleverly divert attention from the real issue.

Self-esteem, in other words, *does not exist*. Self-loathing, however, is very real.

In the classic French film *Jean de Florette*, townspeople in Provence conspire to trick a man out of the property he has just inherited by capping the farm's only source of water, thus starving his crops and ensuring his downfall. Jean strives mightily to haul water to the farm, unaware that it already has an inexhaustible supply just underground.

Similarly, believers in self-esteem strive to import a sense of self-worth, neglecting the fact that no such efforts are really necessary: all they need to do is remove the plug that prevents self-worth from flowing. That plug is the relentless self-criticism in which they engage.

Your mission, then, is to affirm your faith in the concept of self-esteem. Strive to build it up within yourself. Attend workshop after workshop, recite affirmations, invite friends and therapists to exalt your achievements. In doing so, you will reinforce both the hidden conviction that there is much to make up for and the corresponding belief in your inherent faultiness.

Sisyphus found an ideal path to misery: endlessly rolling a stone up a hill, only to have it repeatedly escape his grasp and tumble to the bottom. Trying to create self-esteem is like trying to construct a ladder out of water. Futility leads to unhappiness, and seeing yourself as lacking something that does not actually exist is a perfect example.

PART THREE

Hell Is Other People

If misery loves company, misery has company enough.

—Henry David Thoreau

'Tis the only comfort of the miserable to have partners in their woes.

—Miguel de Cervantes

In Jean-Paul Sartre's play *No Exit*, a man is shown into a nicely appointed hotel room, where he is eventually joined by two others. He understands that he has died and that this is Hell, but there are no obvious means to torment him. Increasingly irritated by interactions with his companions, he comes to realize that the punishment in this place is simple human interaction.

No flames, no boiling oil—just the constant presence of other people. This is torment enough. Sartre, it appears, was not much of an extrovert.

Time for a thought experiment. Mentally list five standout occasions when you were particularly unhappy. Go on. I'll wait.

Now, how many of those situations involved the behavior, presence, absence, or loss of other people?

If you are like the majority, the answer is either "most of them" or "all of them." Social relations are complex, shifting, and impermanent. This makes them potential wellsprings of both happiness and misery. Want to change how you feel? Change how you relate to others.

In this section, then, let's list some of the more potent strategies for creating unhappiness via our relationships. One proviso: I have chosen to bypass a particularly rich vein of possibility— romantic and marital relationships (some see the two as mutually exclusive)—simply because they are so rife with ways to feel worse. No point in shooting fish in a barrel. Besides, some readers are not in such relationships, and it is preferable for all of the strategies in the book to be universally applicable, or as close to that lofty goal as can be achieved. For those wishing to manufacture relationship hell, however, do not despair. Most or all of the techniques listed in this section are easily utilized in the service of turning a perfectly good relationship into misery, abandonment, or both.

Become an Island
unto Yourself

We are a social species. Unlike bears or cougars, we are built to spend our time in groups. Alone on the savannah, we would never have lasted long. For most of human history, we appear to have lived in tribes of seventy-five to 150 people. Those who could not handle the complexity of the relationships would go off on their own. Lions need to eat, after all.

Today we have created a world in which more than half of the population lives in urban areas (over 75 percent in the more developed countries[7]). One would think this would eradicate the unhappiness associated with isolation, but no. It turns out that we were not built to function best in groups of *at least* seventy-five to 150, but in groups *between* seventy-five and 150. There is a cost associated with being in bigger crowds.

For one thing, the complexity of the relationships becomes astronomical as numbers rise. In a group of three people, there are three relationships: A with B, A with C, and B with C. A group of four has six relationships: AB, AC, AD, BC, BD, CD. By the time we get to one hundred there are 4,950 relationships— probably too many to keep track of completely, but still within the firing range of humanity's remarkable social abilities. When we get to a city of just fifty thousand people, however, the total number of relationships is 1,249,975,000—over a billion— incomprehensible to any of us, no matter what our social skills might be. We have to start walling them off.

Not surprisingly, the urban environment is constructed precisely for this purpose. Modern housing developments often present a row of garages to the street, the houses hiding behind them as though sheltering from gunfire. Neighbors cannot see one another, let alone chat from their nonexistent front porches. Residential developments such as these are described with the modern marketing term for isolation: privacy. And indeed, they are private. The first hint that there may be problems next door is likely to be a fence-jumping odor of decaying flesh and some well-fed housecats.

So once again, we have a path to misery that has been cleared, paved, and widened by our culture. You need only choose the on-ramp and accelerate down the road. In his book *Bowling Alone*, Robert Putnam has documented the decline of social groups such as the Rotary Club, churches, and, yes, bowling leagues in Western societies—this at a time of coincident rises in the rates of depression. The temptation to draw a link is overwhelming.

In the years before satellite imagery, the government of British Columbia frequently employed college students to staff mountaintop forest-fire watchtowers through the summers. Much of their time would be spent alone. Now abandoned and crumbling, these towers still sit at the summit of many hiking trails. To many job-hunting students, this seemed like an ideal and somewhat undemanding task. Every year, however, many of them would have to be removed from their posts, desperately unhappy, having discovered that they simply were not cut out to be isolated from the tribe for such an extended period.

It may seem impractical to pursue a strategy of isolation, given that it might appear to require a lonely cabin in the woods or on a mountaintop. Nothing could be further from the truth. As we have discussed, the modern urban environment is built specifically to facilitate isolation. You don't have to do anything at all in order to achieve your goal.

We have managed to create privacy to such an extent that it takes considerable effort for city-dwellers *not* to be isolated. Further, if they remain fixated directly on the goal of meeting people, they can accidentally join us on the path to misery. After all, how do you meet people? They can waltz down the street shaking hands with strangers, but this will only get them startled looks, not admiring friends. The direct approach fails more often than not.

Those wanting to build a larger social network must put the goal of meeting people on a shelf and ask themselves, "What *else* do I want in my life?" Then they must pursue those other interests in such a way that they have human contact as a side effect. They have to join clubs, take night-school classes, schedule outings, do volunteer work, play sports, and generally occupy a significant portion of their time plotting how to find, cultivate, and spend time with small subtribes within the urban crush. If they do not, many find that they can wander the streets of their neighborhoods for days and never run into anyone they know.

The world of the Internet, at first blush, seems designed to overcome isolation. The various social media platforms allow us to connect instantly with innumerable people all over the world. We can build an online tribe based on arcane interests shared by no one in our hometowns. And indeed, some of our yens for contact can be met in this way.

But if you think of the social diet as being composed of various vitamins, some of the most essential ones are missed in online connection—genuineness, nonverbal communication, face-to-face contact, and more. Sit alone in your basement discussing Russian prehistory or, perhaps more likely, killing other people's war-game avatars or watching cat videos, and you will develop a misery-inducing deficiency quite quickly.

So build an island. Put up the fence, close the garage door, switch on the computer, and kid yourself that you have substituted in-the-flesh social contact with the pixelated kind. It is one of the most effective routes to unhappiness that exists.

Give Them What They Want

Imagine that you choose to join humanity rather than isolating yourself. How can you maintain your position within the tribe? People differ. Your combination of wishes, passions, opinions, preferences, and desires is unique, and it will be easy for others to view it as deranged, depraved, or simply inadequate. Even if you were entirely like the others with whom you socialize, some resources are finite. If everyone wants to be the center of attention, someone has to be the audience.

In every relationship between two people, there are two sets of expectations: yours and your friend's. Which should govern your behavior?

One option is to forget all about their priorities and pursue your own without care for what your friend might prefer. Getting little nourishment from interacting with you, however, he will soon leave you solitary once more—and before departing, he will probably dispense a litany of painful criticism. This is one path to misery.

The other option is to set your opinions, wishes, and priorities aside as irrelevant and adopt your friend's instead:

- If she liked the movie, enthuse wildly about it yourself.

- If she wants to visit Baffin Island, then refrain from suggesting Paris.

- If she votes for the Mars First party, claim that you do as well.

Become adept at delaying your reply when (or if) he asks your opinion—at least until you have divined his. Then simply express his preferences as though they were your own. Become what object-relations theorists call a *mirror object*, reflecting back to your partner what he most hopes to see: himself.

This sounds generous and winning—not at all a path to unhappiness—but it is quite effective. For one thing, no matter how much people enjoy looking in mirrors, eventually they get bored and look away. Your friend, colleague, or spouse will realize that she doesn't need to ask your point of view—for some reason, it always mimics hers. Talking to you is like talking to herself, and sooner or later she will need more stimulation than you seem able to provide. Having sacrificed yourself on the altar of her regard, you will find that she has simply lost interest.

In addition, the part of you that requires the nourishment of having your needs met will wither away, leaving you resentful and unhappy. You can relinquish your interests, suppress your point of view, and neglect your needs for an evening, perhaps even for a week. But you cannot do so forever and have your mood sustain itself. Invisible behind the mirror you hold up to the world, you will get no real benefit from the social approval you achieve. It will be like attempting to get a suntan behind a lead shield.

An example often seen in therapy is the young gay or lesbian individuals who go out, socialize, and become involved in the world but stay carefully in the closet, displaying a falsely heterosexual self to others. They may get warm approval for much of what they do, but the heat never quite penetrates to the heart. They sense the affection they would receive if they really were the person they pretend to be, but knowing they are not, they cannot feel the benefit. Hence the value of coming out: as gay, as opinionated, as political, as religious, as atheist, as flawed, as whatever and whoever you happen to be.

We all play roles in the world, and none of us reveals everything. But the more you adopt a disguise, the more you deny yourself; and the more you pretend to be something other than what you are, the more unhappy you are likely to become. In some ways, this can be more painful than simple isolation. Rather than sitting alone at home with a bare cupboard, you find yourself hungrily eyeing a heavily laden smorgasbord locked behind glass.

So think. What are all the aspects of yourself that you could practice hiding away when company comes?

- Your religion (Wicca is so outré).

- Your profession (tell them you're a lawyer, and you'll just hear tired jokes).

- Your politics (heaven forbid they call you a liberal).

- Your sexuality (heterosexuality just seems so restrictive).

- Your hobbies (no one understands stamp collecting any more).

- Your history (a childhood in poverty will surely attract their disdain).

- Your psychopathology (if they know you have OCD, they'll ask you to do the dishes).

- Your family (the performance-artist sister will have them questioning your genetics).

Lock them all away and reveal them to no one, even when you suspect they would not give offense.

Make it your mission to melt into the wallpaper, showing the people in your life only what they see in themselves. Reinforce their points of view. Go along with them like a puppy on a leash. Tell yourself that by stingily withholding your reality, you are being generous, providing them with the space and room to be themselves.

You may sense that you cannot do this forever. You're right about that—you can't. But it doesn't matter. They won't stick around anyway.

LESSON 23

Measure Up and Measure Down

How are you doing, relative to others? Do you measure up? Are you at the top of the heap, in the thick of the pack, or lagging behind?

You know where to place yourself if you want to be miserable. You need to look bad. One solution is genuinely to lag, but this is hard to do on every possible measure. Just when you succeed at berating yourself for your uselessness at volleyball, some cheerful spark within will remind you of your shining knowledge of astrophysics.

Instead, compare yourself to others in such a way that you almost always look worse. There is a fiendishly clever way of doing so that those with an innate talent for self-deprecation learn without knowing they are learning it. Unfortunately, these kinds of machinations tend to work best if you don't know that you are doing them. So if you read the strategy here, you must make its practice as automatic as possible and then forget that you ever heard it.

Imagine that you walk into a party. You have been casually following the recent election campaign, you are moderately competent on the guitar, and you are childishly pleased with the new jacket you are wearing. You look around. In one corner is a group of people chatting about the election, surrounding a party insider who knows intimate details of the polling, the issues, and the candidates. Out on the front porch, Eric Clapton, wearing a stained t-shirt, is strumming a guitar. In the inevitable kitchen crush, one couple is sporting immaculate tailored outfits that radiate cool without appearing obnoxiously flashy.

What do you do?

For maximum misery, spend the evening comparing yourself to others. But—and here's the key—not to everyone. Choose carefully.

Remind yourself that you had made a point of brushing up on the latest political news so you might have something to talk about tonight. Compare your meager knowledge about the election to the obvious expertise of the insider in the corner. You have nothing to add that he doesn't know already. Dwell on the idea that your self-congratulation for being so well informed now looks foolish.

In the back of your mind, you had thought that someone might break out a guitar, and you could impress with your country twelve-string rendition of Lady Gaga's "Poker Face."

Compare this to what Clapton is doing and feel somewhat pathetic by contrast.

Compare your new off-the-rack jacket to the designer clothes of the power couple in the kitchen—you aren't nearly as well dressed.

Keep going. Compare your hair, teeth, age, physical condition, social skills, job, income, travel experience, skill set, spouse, relationship history, friendship network, sense of humor, number of languages spoken, ability to dance, vehicle, choice of beverage, upbringing, education, address, and anything else you can think of with the other people present. It doesn't really matter whether you know all of these details for the people around you. Make assumptions.

But do not compare your clean and new jacket to Clapton's ratty t-shirt, your guitar skills to the tone-deaf political operative, or your election knowledge to the clueless power couple in the kitchen. Every comparison you make must be downward, with you on the bottom end.

Similarly, avoid comparing yourself to the group at large. If you do so, you may come across as better dressed, more musically talented, and better informed than average. You don't know particle physics as well as Stephen Hawking over by the piano, but you seem to grasp the basics about as well as the person next to him. Your slacks are no match for Donatella's leopard prints, but they're fine by the standards of the group. This will not aid you in your quest.

Instead, choose the person representing the high end of the continuum on every variable, and compare yourself to them:

- Select the person with the single best haircut and feel like a slob.

- Find the owner of the Lamborghini and feel humiliated by your old beater.

- Listen to the amateur sommelier exclaim over the mushroom notes in the wine and tell yourself that you are hopelessly unsophisticated by comparison.

You don't have to wait for a party invitation. You can do this anytime: at work, in meetings, walking down the street, in restaurants, meeting up with friends, watching people on television, or even just sitting alone at home. If you find it difficult, you might try specializing in a few categories: your weight, your thinning hair, your income, your inability to cook sambal green beans.

Practice downward comparisons with those few characteristics until you have perfected the art. Then you can branch out, generalize, and make yourself feel globally inadequate.

Sometimes you'll realize that you are indeed at the bottom of the pack. All of these people are marathoners, and you haven't jogged in decades. Carefully avoid reminding yourself of your other qualities. While they were out running, you were raising children and learning bookkeeping. These observations will only lessen the sting. You must also avoid replacing envy with admiration. Feel crushed by their achievements, not inspired by them.

Should these downward comparisons prove beyond your talents at self-abasement, the opposite strategy may be easier. Find the person with the worst example of each characteristic instead. The poorest diction. The silliest look. The lamest jokes. Cultivate a feeling of smug superiority over them. You might think that this would make you feel happy, but no. Your attitude will seep into your interactions with others, and they will gently drift away, leaving you alone once more.

Play to Win

At the Atlanta Olympics in 1996, controversy erupted over a running-shoe advertisement on local transit. Its tagline read, "You don't win silver—you lose gold." This implied a remarkable point of view. You might master your sport, rise to excellence, become one of the best in your country, be accepted to the Olympics, and perform to within a centimeter of the most accomplished athletes there. And that would make you a loser. A failure.

That copywriter should be your hero.

A competitive stance toward social interaction is a stunningly effective strategy for the production of misery. You and a hundred of your relatives, friends, or coworkers might work at a project or attend an event—but only one of you will rise to the top. The others will head home as failures. Most of the time, of course, you will be among them.

Sometimes it's especially easy to turn an activity into a competition. You are on the squash ladder at your fitness center. You run a footrace. You strive for the "Employee of the Month" award. You fight to get the corner office. In all of these instances, it's obvious who wins, and if there were more than two in the battle, it usually won't be you.

In many social situations, however, the winner is less clear. Who comes away with the gold medal from a dinner party, a camping trip, a drive to the beach, a discussion about oil-development policy?

Here the best strategy is to take events in which there is no obvious rivalry and create one. Who can prepare the best dish, start a campfire with the fewest matches, get to the beach fastest, prove their point about oil? Compare your efforts to theirs, insist that you are right and they are wrong, and challenge them to a race or test.

This can be hard work. Most people aren't wired to see everything as a win-or-lose game. After all, does knowing more about Ecuador really make you superior? Does humiliating your nephews at checkers gain their affection? If someone has a more discerning nose for wine, does this make her more sophisticated or does it just mean she drinks too much?

Getting people who raise questions like this to compete is like tossing a ball to a dog that just wants to go back to sleep. You may have to goad them to the starting line. One option is to imply that they fear competing with you or lack the requisite killer instinct ("C'mon, ya chicken!"). Another is to imply that they would lose anyway and that their reluctance to compete constitutes a loss before the race has begun ("You know I'm fastest").

If they still won't bite, compete anyway. Prove your point until they drift away. Run whether she follows or not. Argue until he stops phoning. The transitory sense of superiority that you achieve will ferment with the yeast of loneliness into a potent sense of unhappy futility. And if you do manage to entice them to compete and then lose to them, you can add your own humiliation to the mix.

Ensure that your compatriots do not view the competition as trivial, good natured, or fun:

- If you are swimming and race them to the dock, examine their faces. Did they enjoy the effort regardless of how they fared?

- When you point out the blackberry notes in the wine, do they appreciate the insight or look embarrassed to have missed them?

- When you humorlessly prevent them from winning a single hand of cards, do they still enjoy your company?

True victory means they should see its significance—that you are the superior creature—and they should want to abandon the field to you.

Doesn't this run the risk of happiness? In a field of lackadaisical contestants who would rather enjoy each other's company than get in a test of one-upmanship, mightn't you win and be triumphant? Only briefly. In 279 BCE, King Pyrrhus remarked after winning a costly skirmish, "If we are victorious in one more battle with the Romans, we shall be utterly ruined."[8] Similarly, any victory you achieve will be Pyrrhic—you will win the race but lose their respect, prove your point but be proven foolish.

Competition may nevertheless seem to be the path to triumphant happiness, so my casting it as a route to misery may seem suspect. Look carefully at the reflexively competitive individuals around you, however, and you will see a deeply driven nail of shame—partly the source of their competitive style, partly the result of it.

The real happiness-inducing prize is having a group of people who feel positively toward you, who include you on the invitation list, and who feel better because you were there. None of these goals are served by proving your imaginary superiority. You may be able to win the war, but the troops you conquer will be your own.

I once attempted to treat a man with a distinctly competitive approach to the world. To him, every encounter produced a winner and a loser. Even therapy. All of my attempts to put him in the driver's seat, to support him in making changes he wanted to make, and to get on his side failed miserably. He saw our encounters as a battle between us and could not be persuaded otherwise. Knowing that my secret goal was for him to be contented in his life, he pulled the other way. And, given that his life was in his own hands all along, of course he won. And so can you.

Nature is red in tooth and claw. So should you be.

Hold High
Expectations of Others

Your chances of achieving a truly saddening isolation are much enhanced if the pool of potential friendship candidates is exceedingly small. To accomplish this, all you need do is set the inclusion threshold high. Create a mental or, better still, a written list of your criteria for your friends, acquaintances, and partners. Narrow the highway of your acceptance to a knife's edge.

Perhaps to be worthy of your regard, people must

- hold your political views and vote for the same party;

- use the same social media you do;

- be within x years of your own age;

- share your religion, ethnicity, sexual orientation, and national origin;

- approximate your level of education and occupational attainment;

- live on a convenient transit line;

- occupy the upper quartile of the population in terms of physical attractiveness or income;

- be related to you (or be unrelated to you);

- have the same recreational interests, taste in music, fashion sense, and percentage of adipose tissue; and

- part their hair on the left.

This all but ensures that your social circle will be small. Do the math. Of a thousand randomly selected people from your community, how many share all of the above, and more (your opinion of cruise ships, your feelings about retirement, your love of birdwatching)? Watch how quickly your winnowing reduces the numbers. A thousand people are not enough; you are down to fractions within moments.

Become a truly discerning connoisseur of humanity, and you will eliminate virtually everyone from candidacy. If a tiny number remains, you can face a troubling prospect. Relationships are two-way. How likely is it that you measure up to their standards as well? If one in a thousand meets your exacting standards, and if he or she is as choosy as you, then approval will be mutual with only one in a million people.

Even if you do manage to find a social network this way, misery is likely. By marking out an insurmountable division between acceptable and unacceptable individuals, you can create the cozily claustrophobic sensation of being "we few, we lucky few" against the marauding inhuman hordes outside your social network—a feeling mimicked by films about the housebound survivors of zombie plagues.

It is seldom possible to sit one's social candidates down for a truly extensive screening interview. Consequently, as you learn more about people, you will discover that most of them cross the line in one way or another, thus falling into the "unacceptable" camp. When this occurs, get rid of them. The discomfort of watching your circle shrink further (and the acrimony of their social ejection) may further darken your disposition. You can then spend solitary months gnawing on your resentment like a shih tzu with a twist of rawhide. *They weren't the people I thought they were.*

Even if your friends and family do manage to pass your tests (a fact that alone should tell you that your standards are regrettably lax), you can demand top performance in their day-to-day interactions with you. Set high expectations for such imponderables as their generosity, the speed with which they respond to your e-mail, the timing of birthday acknowledgments, their ability to divine your good intentions without outward cues, and so on.

Above all, expect your associates to tolerate in you what you would never tolerate in them. Do not just hold them to the same standards you set for yourself. Set their bar much higher than your own. Whereas you are free to forget lunch dates, ignore their pleas for support, neglect birthdays, and turn conversations into lengthy monologues, insist that for them to do so would be a cardinal sin.

To help out, psychologists have invented the brilliantly destructive concept of *unconditional positive regard*. This is the belief that one's feelings of affection should be constant and unwavering regardless of the behavior of the other person. Demand this of everyone you meet. To quote a recent "motivational" Internet meme, "Do not stay where you are tolerated; go only where you are celebrated."

The genius of unconditional positive regard is that it is entirely mythological—something that even parents cannot wholeheartedly sustain for their children. Your friends will be unable to muster it on your behalf, and you will find yourself unable to produce it in return—thus enabling you to feel simultaneously aggrieved and inadequate.

LESSON 26

Drop Your Boundaries

Perhaps you are unsuited to the narcissistic role of demanding that others live up to your standards. No problem. You can try to live up to theirs instead. Whatever the relationship—familial, friendship, romantic, work related—you can make it your goal to satisfy the demands of the people around you. If they tell you to jump, you can say, "Pardon me for asking, and I know I should have paid closer attention to instructions previously, but how high?"

For this to have the maximum effect, the best people to have in your social group should be those for whom the previous strategy ("Hold High Expectations of Others") comes naturally. You want to collect people who adopt exacting and inflexible standards—the demanding, hard-to-satisfy types who are unaware that few could measure up to their expectations and who are therefore scornful of all those who fail.

The core element of the strategy is to eliminate the word *no* from your vocabulary:

- If your friend wants you to skip work to drive her to the airport, do it.

- If your spouse expects you to make the meals, clean the house, take care of the children, work a full-time job, and then praise him for working as hard as he does, do so.

- If your son expects you not only to make his meals, but also to deliver them, warm, to the side table by his computer, start cooking.

- If, on Christmas Eve, your boss drops a load of work on your desk as she sails out the door to her ski chalet, stay late and get it done.

Whatever they desire—favors, money, work, a blind eye to their indiscretions—give it.

The nice thing about this strategy is that it does not require the learning of any new skills. In fact, the people who are the best at it are those who have never mastered the art of setting interpersonal boundaries. The inability to say no is one of the primary hallmarks of the passive mode of communication, which places other people firmly in charge of your own life.

How does this produce misery? Let me count the ways.

First, it cultivates in others the expectation that you will fulfill their every demand—making you a cross between a scullery maid and a genie. This causes them to increase their expectations over time. Soon they will expect more than you can possibly deliver and will be just as enraged as they would be if, at the outset, you had flatly refused their simple request to pass the butter.

Second, by practicing this role with many people at once, you can create steadily increasing circles of personal responsibility that eventually intersect. Next Tuesday, for example, your mother wants a ride to her dental appointment, your son wants to borrow the car, and your best friend demands an afternoon confab about her impending divorce. The rules you have chosen for yourself dictate that you cannot say no to any of them. It's possible to stickhandle a few of these situations, but eventually you will be entirely overcommitted. The balls you have volunteered to juggle will plop to the ground, and your audience will pounce on your failure.

Third, any remaining time you have for your own needs will be steadily whittled down to nothing. The activities that sustain you (exercising, eating, sleeping) will have to be relinquished.

Fourth, you will reinforce a perception of yourself as being deserving of this treatment. A part of your mind always watches your own behavior, like a hidden observer trying to understand your role. Seeing you routinely subvert your own interests to pander to others' whims, that portion of your brain will conclude that you are worth less than others, and you will develop (or intensify) a corresponding feeling of inferiority.

The easiest way to maintain this strategy until it bites especially deeply is simply to avoid learning any principles for the setting and maintaining of interpersonal boundaries. Another route is to tell yourself that you shouldn't *have* to have any of these skills. Others should be more considerate. No matter how hard you try to hide it, no matter how many times you say, "No, really, it's just fine. I'd be glad to," they should read your exhaustion and limit their requests.

They, of course, will rely on your agreement rather than on their nonexistent telepathic powers and take you at your word— or at your behavior. If you hand them money, then it will seem obvious that you are willing to offer the loan; asking was not the wrong thing to do.

You need never worry that they will stop asking or stepping across the lines that you have spent a lifetime erasing from their view. The requests will go on escalating—and their spurs will dig ever deeper—unless you make the mistake of stepping forward and taking the reins from their hands.

This strategy is easy to adopt in part because resentment is seductive. A part of us *likes* to feel aggrieved at the unreasonable demands of other people. We enjoy the comforting self-pity of being nailed to the cross and don't like to see that we are the ones holding the hammer.

After all, what's the alternative? In order to adopt the assertive posture, we would have to remove our blinders and gaze into the glare of uncomfortable truth. Our life isn't really under anyone else's control. We are in the saddle.

We tell ourselves that others are the problem, so they are the ones who have to change. But we can't change them (despite our efforts), so we're stuck. Real control would mean relinquishing attempts to change them and changing our own behavior instead. We could say no. We need not stamp our feet, get red in the face, or scream in frustration. We could simply smile calmly and state our position:

- "I'd love to take you to the airport, but I'm at work until six that day."

- "No, I'm using the car tomorrow."

- "I'll be glad to serve dinner the moment the garbage is out."

- "I can't stop you from having another affair, but if you do, I'll be leaving."

This frightening prospect is the road, ultimately, to greater happiness with one's life, though in the short term the people around us would object, and probably wouldn't take us seriously. You've said things like this before, after all, and then you backed down. When confronted with a newly installed boundary, people always test its strength. If you were to stand your ground and do what you told them you would do, they would eventually get the message that your life is your own, and that you were taking charge of it.

Best not risk that, however. It's easier just to follow instructions.

Bond with People's Potential, Not Their Reality

One way to ensure your own unhappiness is to form relationships with purely hypothetical people. This is not as difficult as it sounds, because you don't have to hallucinate the flesh and blood. The raw materials are all around you, in the shapes of the people in your life.

People are inherently flawed, however. Look closely enough at your friends, your family members, your coworkers, or your partner, and you will see ample room for improvement. Almost anyone could be a bit better with a nip here, a tuck there, a change in personality, a nicer job, a spiffier haircut, an altered habit or two. It is this idealized image that you should bond with, not the person's current manifestation.

Here's the strategy:

- Find a person (male or female, but a flip of the coin makes him male for our example) whom you don't really like all that much—at least not as he is.

- Believe that within him you can see the raw materials of a truly wonderful person.

- Begin a friendship or romance.

- Fool him into believing that you are attracted to his present incarnation, not a fantasy of the future.

- Once he's hooked, take out your carpentry kit and get started on the renovation.

Put yourself to work caring for the person, tending to his needs, and subverting your own. Spend so much time and effort that you create a debt he can only repay by changing. Keep this accounting in your own mind, without letting him know about it. Tell yourself that the vacuum of his own contributions will eventually seep into his consciousness and, inspired by your selfless example, he will (select one): (a) give up drinking, (b) get a job, (c) go back to school, (d) learn some manners, (e) end his criminality, (f) treat you properly, (g) stop sleeping around, or (h) learn to take care of himself.

Needless to say, this will not happen. You are working from a contract he has not seen and would not sign, and you have never made the terms of the relationship clear. He will interpret your loving care as acceptance of him as he is. If anything, his motivation to change will fade, not grow. This will permit you to become resentful: here you are, slaving away for him, and he does nothing in return.

Eventually you should let the resentment boil over and, like a mayor unveiling a new statue, pull the sheet aside and reveal your true motivations in an angry rant. "I did all this only because I thought you were going to change!" He will be surprised and appalled and will react with anger. "What do you mean—I should quit drinking? You've been the one running to the liquor store ever since I lost my driver's license!"

Even if you have been clear all along that you think a bit of monogamy might be fun or that drug dealing is not an ideal long-term career choice, your actions will have spoken louder than your words. You stayed. Obviously—at least in the mind of the other person—you did not really want the change all that much or you did not really expect it.

Furthermore, the time you have spent on your involuntary rehabilitation project will have enabled you to distract yourself from the issues percolating in your own life. Starved for attention, your problems will have become more pressing and intractable. This will make them more difficult to resolve and will, coincidentally, provide your friend or partner with ammunition for their defensive position. "Look at you! You're hardly an example of perfect mental health yourself!" The person's benign tolerance for your self-neglect will give him—or her—a rationale for not changing to suit you, and the problem can continue.

Does all this seem too taxing? You can always try out a much watered-down version in any close relationship. Try to make your spouse, child, parent, roommate, or best friend change on just a few small variables. Anything will do. The worldwide favorites are lateness versus promptness and messiness versus order.

Harangue your organizationally challenged husband to get to places on time or your overly busy wife to use the laundry hamper. Firmly refuse to change your expectations or behavior. Surely it is your spouse's issue, not yours, so it is up to him or her to change. The fact that your spouse feels tyrannized by your enslavement to the clock or your overly fussy sense of sterility ("Oh, is *Architectural Digest* coming for a photo shoot?") is only defensiveness on their part.

You could, if your standards were lower, accept your friends' or family members' flaws. Rather than urging them to be different, you could accommodate them:

- Your "late" husband? You could try to make him as time conscious as you are—and fume every time you stand, drenched, waiting for him at a rainy street corner. Alternatively, you could give up and change yourself instead—perhaps by telling him that you will meet him inside the restaurant rather than out on the street.

- Laundry is your chore, and your wife refuses to use the hamper? You could go on haranguing her to change. Or you could wash whatever you find in the hamper and ignore the bras on the floor nearby.

- Your friend is notoriously bad with money? You could lecture him about how simple it is, or you could just refrain from making him the club treasurer.

If you were to end the power struggle, change might actually happen. Slowly. Over time. But it would not happen because of your fantasy or to suit you. Indeed, by demanding that grown adults conform to your vision, you may be placing a roadblock in the way of their change, thus ensuring your misery. In order to remain autonomous, they must resist all of your efforts to reform them.

These battles will never be won, so you need not concern yourself that the brick wall, with repeated forehead strikes, will one day give way. It will go on providing you with the joys of futile effort forever. Sisyphus would be so pleased.

Demand Loyalty

Quick—think of the last three social events you attended. Anything at all: a wedding, a night at the pub, dinner at someone's home, a walk in the park with a friend, a chat by the water cooler. Why did you participate? Select one:

- because you wanted and chose to do it—it was tempting, or you believed that it would prove enjoyable, that it would expand your range of experiences, or that it fit with your personal values

- because of a sense of duty, guilt, and indebtedness to the people you would be seeing

The first option accounts for the majority of most people's social encounters. Even if we include events such as funerals, we often go because we want to attend, pay our respects, and comfort the family—rather than out of a sense of resentful, foot-dragging obligation.

Sometimes there are a few events in the second category as well—times when we put in an appearance mainly to avoid disapproval for not attending, or as part of a social trade-off. Your spouse attended your company's Christmas party, so you go to his or her departmental summer barbecue. Fine. Of course, etiquette in these situations often demands that the motives be disguised. "I didn't want to come, because your dinners are so boring, but I felt I must" is seldom the kickoff to a sparkling evening.

Using the principle that others are, in many respects, like us, we can conclude that most people socialize with us because they *want* to do so, not because they *should*—and that if they came out of obligation, they might not really be fully present in any case. A hidden, inward part of them would be at home watching the hockey game.

When we find ourselves tempted to ask, "Why don't you ever visit (or call or write or invite me to dinner)?" we could use this as a cue to turn the situation around and answer our own question. Why don't they? We could put ourselves in the role of our companion and replay the last few encounters. What would those evenings have been like? How enjoyable would they have been?

Doing this, we can sometimes become uncomfortably aware that we are relying far more on the other person's loyalty than on our own role in the exchange. We were drunk or critical or late or inconsiderate or monopolizing or silent or selfish or manipulative—and it would be difficult for anyone to have said that the time spent with us was enjoyable.

This route to unhappiness involves assuming the opposite: that people seek you out due to a feeling of obligation—out of a belief that they *should* do so, not because they anticipate a pleasant exchange or a positive outcome. No matter who it is—friends, siblings, a spouse—you should believe and assert that they should invite you out, drop by, or engage you in conversation simply because you have a relationship with them, not because they anticipate the exchange to produce any of the myriad forms of human enjoyment.

Demand this from them. In fact, demand more. Expect them to share your political views, tolerate your narcissistic self-focus, and defend you without question to anyone who voices their displeasure with you. Expect them to behave with you the way you would like to believe you do with them. Award yourself extra points if you can come up with a good rationale dictating why they should be even *more* loyal to you than you are to them.

The great thing about this strategy is that it absolves us from examining our own role in the relationship. When there is no knock at the door, we are free to rehearse our resentment at their inconsideration without having to look in an unflattering mirror.

Surely, you are tempted to say, *surely* we can find misery both ways. By putting the responsibility squarely on their shoulders, we can savor our embitterment. And by examining ourselves we can feel inadequate and offensive, and we can embark upon a session of self-criticism and self-loathing. But take the next step in the chess game. Understanding our own role in the problem, we might choose to become better companions. No such risk awaits us if we blame others entirely. We will confront them for their fickleness, make our next encounter with them even less pleasant, and magnify the problem—potentially until they abandon us altogether.

If you can master this strategy, you will be in good company: thousands of friendships—and families—are dissolved in precisely this fashion.

Parents of adult children often use this technique. They seek to increase the frequency of visits with their offspring through the generous use of guilt:

- "I haven't heard from you in sooooo long."

- "I thought you were dead!"

- "Why don't you ever call? Don't you love me?"

Aware of long-ago nights changing their child's diapers and tending them when they were ill, they dwell on the accumulated debt that they perceive their son or daughter has built up, and they wonder when it will all be repaid.

The answer, of course, is never. Grown children are all too aware of the mountain of debt they owe their parents—and the futility of attempting to pay it off. When have any of their parents' friends ever said to their own children: "Consider us even—you no longer have to do anything for me"? Never. Parental sacrifice is a thousand-year mortgage. It can never be paid off, so many offspring feel it's pointless to try.

If these frustrated parents were to shift their gaze onto their own behavior, it might suddenly become no great mystery why their child never calls, writes, or visits. The interactions are so suffused with guilt, anxiety, and manipulation that positive feelings are snuffed out completely. Some empty nesters could give lessons in how to ensure that a child moves away as far as possible and loses the ability to telecommunicate.

"But wait," comes the objection. "I don't have to entertain them. They're my family and friends. If I can't be myself with them, who can I relax with?" Sadly, if being oneself means becoming a fountain of guilt, unsolicited advice, ill-disguised criticism, or outright hostility, the answer is clear. No one.

Of course, sooner or later we will be bed-bound with a cracked jaw, unable to speak, make canapés, or perhaps even listen to their problems. Fine. By that time, we may have enough money in the relationship bank that we can make the occasional withdrawal. It is only if we make withdrawals continually without ever making a deposit that we can claim to have mastered the misery-inducing art of alienation.

React to Their Motives, Not Their Messages

In *The Imitation Game*, a biopic about Alan Turing, the father of modern computing, a school friend proffers the young Alan a book about codes and cyphers. He explains that codes are "messages that anyone can see, but no one knows what they mean unless you have the key." Confused, the socially challenged genius says, "How is that different from talking? When people talk to each other, they never say what they mean. They say something else. And you're supposed to just know what they mean. Only I never do."

Communication is inherently difficult for all of us, not just Turing. Just look at what's involved:

- Person A experiences an internal state—a thought, an idea, a mood—that is invisible to Person B.

- Desiring to express this state, Person A imagines what might be required for Person B to get the message accurately—based largely on Person A's own unique history, cultural background, and ideas about "what most people understand."

- Person A encodes the resulting message into language, choosing vocabulary, sentence structure, and the amount of detail to include.

- The message must then be expressed audibly and coherently. At the same time, Person A gives off a complex second set of messages via nonverbal behavior—messages that may agree with or contradict the verbal message.

- Person B must hear the words and see the nonverbals—not always an easy task.

- Person B imposes meaning on the series of sounds using B's own unique history, cultural background, and experiences—many of which do not match those of Person A.

- Nonverbals are interpreted with reference to Person B's own cultural norms and the behavior of people Person B has known before.

- Person B compares and attempts to integrate the verbal and nonverbal messages but does so without the benefit of conscious oversight, resulting in a whole that is often ambiguous. *Hmm, he says he loves me, but he's turning away and looking over my shoulder.*

- The actual message is then decoded into a guess about Person A's actual internal state.

The fact that every discussion doesn't quickly devolve into confusion is a miracle. The messages we receive are seldom exact replicas of the messages that were sent. They are a blend of the intended meaning and the distortions produced by our own hopes and fears about what the person really meant. Our interpretations slide in so readily and automatically that it's easy to miss them. This affords us a perfect opportunity for the creation of unhappiness.

One strategy is to presume that what we heard is what the other person intended to say. This alone is sufficient to create reams of confusion and discord.

No need to stop there, however. Rather than sticking with the words spoken, we can put on our Sherlock Holmes hat and use the message as a starting point for a deep interpretation of the other person's meaning, motives, and overall personality. With every interpretive step away from the actual words of the message, we create more room for distortion. Error after error will creep in, until the meaning we think we are responding to is entirely of our own making.

When a friend asks for the salt in that particularly quiet way, for example, you can convince yourself that she has revealed her intense dislike of you—as well as her general snobbishness— when in reality she is just shy. And you're off and running:

- Having altered and inflated her message, you can react—not to what was said, but to your guesses about her motives or nature. "I can't believe that you have so little respect for me."

- The other person will then react with confusion, failing to understand the relation between what she said and how you responded. "Umm, what?"

- Then you can interpret her incomprehension as passive-aggressive denial. "Don't play dumb. I know what you really think."

- She can become angry at being found guilty of an unknown and unintended crime. "You're accusing me of something, but I don't know what."

- Then her anger will justify your own. "You're upset because I can see through you."

The lovely forest of your friendship will have been set aflame, and you can warm your hands as it burns to ashes.

The closer the relationship, the greater the opportunity for misunderstandings and unhappiness. You can tell yourself with assurance that you truly know the other person, so you can believe in your interpretations even more than you ordinarily would.

Married couples, for example, frequently come to know one another so well that they stop checking their understanding with each other. Two sailboats on virtually the same course—only a single degree's difference on the compass—will be thousands of miles apart after a few years. The result is that long-term couples often have tremendous faith in their understanding of the other person, when in reality they understand their spouse less than they do the plumber.

One of the maxims used by relationship therapists is, "Whatever the argument is about is not really what it's about." A dispute over emptying the cat litter has nothing to do with the cat litter—it's about whether one feels valued or important. Half of marital therapy is getting each partner in turn to listen while the other has a chance to fully express his or her thoughts and feelings. The revelations about what's *really* going on inside one another can often produce the greatest progress.

So if it is your goal to be less happy, consider this your license to over-interpret. Don't check out people's meaning or intent. Assume you know it already, and react accordingly. Here are some signs that you are doing well:

- You frequently discover that people you once liked turn out to seem inconsiderate, disrespectful, or manipulative "users."

- People often say to you, "I don't understand what you're angry about" or "I didn't mean it that way."

- You realize (or are told) that people are tiptoeing
  around you out of a concern about the opinion you
  might develop of them.

You can't really read minds. But if you want misery, don't
stay in your own head. Guess what they meant, and then act on
it. It's like setting a match to gasoline.

LESSON 30

Cultivate and Treasure Toxic Relationships

It can be exhausting to polish your negative filter day in and day out, constantly snipping away unwelcome intrusions of joy and self-worth only to see them grow back like fingernails.

One solution is to subcontract the work. Collect people around you who, one way or another, serve to lower your mood. Here are some candidates:

Insulters. People who are utterly unimpressed by you and make their displeasure clear and constant. The best are those who focus on immutable characteristics of your nature: you are stupid, worthless, ugly, awkward, incompetent, and selfish. If they emphasized your actual behavior, then you could evaluate their implicit recommendations for any worth they might have (*Hmm, maybe I* could *take over the driving more often*), but they don't. You want people whose criticism is

- phrased in the negative (about what you aren't, not about what you could become), and

- about traits that cannot be changed ("short people are a pain").

Bigots are a wonderful resource for this ("white people are so pasty"; "Christians are fools"; "deaf people never listen"), but there are plenty of equal-opportunity critics on the market as well.

Complainers. Whether directing their dissatisfaction toward you or not, these individuals can suck the air out of a stadium. They can find the inadequacies in any situation, so if you stick by their side, you will be treated to their point of view on any experiences you share. The traffic was a nightmare, the restaurant was poorly lit, the movie afterward was spoiled when the microphone appeared in the frame, and the popcorn (which neither of you really needed) was criminally salty.

Nothing is good enough, and nothing can be celebrated. If you viewed the Taj Mahal together, they would point out the cracks in the marble while complaining of the heat.

Underminers. These are individuals who dig away at your pet projects and enthusiasms, showing the ennui and pointlessness lying not too far beneath the surface. "You'll never really finish that novel, and anyway, publishing is a dying business." "Smoking is impossible to give up—here, have one with me." "You're my only friend who still uses crack cocaine, so don't desert me now; I'll buy." "If he doesn't get you a card for every month's anniversary, you should dump him." "You can diet tomorrow." "At our age, you'll never get in shape anyway."

Saboteurs. In workplaces, these individuals operate behind the scenes to deflate enthusiasm, slow projects down, and point out injustices—real or imagined. Seeing themselves as independent thinkers (as opposed to robotic yes-men, of whom you, they imply, appear to be one), they relentlessly emphasize the negative in every endeavor, sowing dissatisfaction and pointless rebellion. The world needs people to point out the downside of things, of course ("Perhaps cutting back on aircraft maintenance is a bit short-sighted"), but true saboteurs go far beyond this and act out their personal resentments rather than providing needed balance.

Narcissists. These are folks who don't need relationships, they need an audience—and you're it. Everything is about their life, their interests, and their needs. Better at monologue than conversation, they show little sign of interest in anything about you—or even that you exist. Your job is to bask in their sunlight, reassuring them that the heat they give off is genuine.

No one can escape having at least a few of these individuals around, but the true seeker of the depths should populate his or her social network with as many of them as possible. Like a hot-air balloon threatening always to break free and soar upward, you want a multitude holding your ropes, anchoring you to the dirt.

But how do we prevent ourselves from activating the ejector seat? With kindness and a reluctance to rock the boat. Hope, like crabgrass, springs eternal. When faced with these toxic people, we can urge ourselves to be patient. Maybe they're having a bad day—or decade. We ourselves are not uniformly good company when life seems to be against us.

Resist the urge to try to help toxic people. It is often tempting to offer a meta-comment: an observation about the person's style of interaction. "Sara, when we're together, you talk a lot about the people you dislike and seldom about people you appreciate." "Rod, you point out a lot you don't like about me. Is there anything you *do* like?" "There are things about this company that I have a hard time with, Margot, but others I support. What keeps you here?"

We're often prevented from making confrontations like this by the fear that we will damage the relationship. Doug, having been confronted by his relentless focus on himself, might not want us around any more. If we think carefully about it, however, we can realize that this isn't much of a price to pay.

We also fear being rude. Other people haven't told Mordecai that they find his negativity stifling; why should we be the first? Sometimes, though, good manners can be damaging—leaving Mordecai to wonder why it is that people head for the exits when he appears. The kinder thing can be to gently point out the reasons for his ever-shrinking network. He may respond with hurt or anger, but he can choose what to do with the information.

Gambits such as these may prove helpful or not, depending on your willingness to follow them up with a clear and patient discussion and on your friends' openness to your feedback. Often, however, their style will prove intractable, and ejection will become tempting. This is an option for those seeking a better life.

If, instead, your quest for ennui is a serious one, talk yourself into keeping them around. Use guilt on yourself to stay attentive: *I owe them gratitude.* Or pity: *They're so unhappy; they need me.* Or pride: *No one else is strong enough to stand them.*

All of your friends and family will fit one or more of the descriptions above for at least part of their lives, as will we. In recognition of this fact, we will want to stand with them out of honor, kindness, and an awareness of the more positive aspects of their nature. But for true misery, you should collect the unremitting, unapologetic, and determined negative influences around you. Exclude the passengers who want to join you in soaring to higher latitudes.

Stick with the ones who hammer you to the ground.

PART FOUR

Living a Life
Without Meaning

I think we're miserable partly because we have only one god,
and that's economics.

—James Hillman

For thousands of years, the world's greatest thinkers have addressed the question of the meaning of life. No clear consensus has emerged.

If they can't resolve this issue, what are *your* chances? It's probably best to give up.

People who have a sense of meaning and purpose in their existence are generally found to have greater life satisfaction than those who don't. Troll the shelves of your local bookstore, and you will find dozens of guides to the purpose-driven life.

So if it is your goal to score in the single digits of any life-satisfaction measure, a sense of purpose should be avoided at all costs. That can sound easy, as if all you have to do is not read any of those books. But just as misery can sneak up on you, so too can a sense of deeper meaning. You will need to be more vigilant—and adopt the meaning-free life deliberately rather than accidentally.

In this section, then, let's take the road less traveled, and look at a subject that few have examined carefully: how to reduce or eliminate a sense of meaning from your life. The journey to misery can be a long one, and we want to free ourselves from any buoyant baggage that might prevent a full exploration of life's murky depths.

For us, the dark night of the soul will not be sufficient. We want to eradicate the dawn forever.

Keep Your Eye on the Small Picture

Unless you are in a race, sailing is a fairly leisurely affair. You sit, you chat, you eat, and you fiddle with ropes. It's easy to allow the boat to become your reference point and your world.

Typically, though, you have a destination in mind. In order to get there, you have to figure out where it is, your present location relative to that one, and the heading you need to be on to get there. The course you take may zigzag so that you can take advantage of the vagaries of the wind. Sometimes the bow will point straight at your goal. More often, you will head to the left or the right, port or starboard, where there is an opportunity for speed, then tack back the other way, always moving (though often tangentially) toward your goal.

Misery in sailing is easy. Don't look where you're going. Soon you'll be on the rocks.

The same principle can be applied to life. Most people don't have an instinctive, automatic sense of their ultimate priorities, any more than a sailor knows where the harbor is without glancing at the horizon. We are unlikely to reach or embody our life's goals or values unless we have some inkling what they are.

For those wishing to homestead at the very bottom of the emotional valley, it is possible to know one's core values and simply neglect to put them into practice. It is better still, however, if the values themselves remain obscure.

In order to prevent the appearance of a tiresome sense of meaning in your life, it is best to avoid contemplating the bigger questions of life—such as these:

- What would you be doing if your life were important?

- If you were living your real life, what would that look like?

- What would you do if you took your life seriously?

- What would you do if you had only one more year to live?

Those wanting a heading for their lives quickly discover that it is difficult to answer any of these questions while scrubbing the toilet, sitting in a meeting, or waiting for a traffic light to change. Replies appear only when the mind slows and pulls itself away from the distractions of the moment. It is necessary to set aside time, sit back, and give one's undivided attention to the task—without intermittently checking for new e-mail, indulging idle fantasies, or listening for the washing machine to click off.

This makes it easy to remain in the dark about any bigger vision for your life: simply stay busy. Involve yourself as much as you can in the activities of the moment, slotting in task after task to follow the one you happen to be working on, so there is never time for wide-ranging contemplation. Rather than stepping back to examine the shape of your life's forest as a whole, remain fixated on the bark of the individual tree before you.

Should questions like those listed above enter your mind, feel free to entertain them—but only when your attention is split between introspection and some other chore. Without the full wattage of your brain, you need not worry that you will arrive at a life-enhancing realization.

If, despite your best efforts—or as a result of prior self-examination—you *do* know what your life could be about, all is not lost. Mind your own busy-ness. Lose yourself once more in the endless detail of life and do not act on any aspect of your goals or values.

If, for example, care of the environment is important to you, ensure that you use this only to fuel your resentment and despair. Do nothing to contribute in a positive way. Donate neither time nor money, and live in a way that repudiates your goal (perhaps seeing just how big an environmental footprint your lifestyle can create).

Your top priority should be to prevent the shining sword of realization from rising out of the lake into your awareness. But if it does, ignore it and behave as though it weren't there. Given a bit of time, Excalibur will once again sink beneath the waves, perhaps forever.

Let Your Impulses Be Your Guide

How should you decide what to do this evening? You could open the mail, call a friend, clean up the hall closet, turn on the television, open a beer—or any of a hundred other activities.

Think of what your emotional state would be at three separate times during the course of any action—let's say, heading to the gym:

- You might feel something ahead of time, contemplating the thought of going to the gym tonight.

- You would feel something while you were there.

- Then you would feel something else as you returned home.

For any event you can feel something beforehand, during, and afterward.

These feelings often don't match up. If you're like most people, the anticipation of exercise is not particularly appealing. *Ugh, I'd rather do anything else.* While you're there perhaps it isn't great, but it's not horrible. Afterward, most people find that they are glad they exercised. If we boil down the complexity of emotion into positives and negatives, the before-during-after sequence is negative-neutral-positive.

What about giving up on the gym and flicking channels on the television instead? It's powerfully tempting; the television is right there, and it's so much easier than getting organized to get some exercise. While you're watching, there's usually a grinding sense of dissatisfaction. *How can there be nothing on?* Afterward, there may be the regret of yet another wasted evening. Positive-negative-negative.

What you decide to do depends mainly on which emotion you use as your guide: temptation beforehand, enjoyment during, or satisfaction afterward. If misery is your goal, the answer is simple. Follow your gut. Base your decision on the temptation that you feel ahead of time.

Most things that will elevate your mood bring relatively little anticipatory desire: exercise, eating healthy food, getting to bed on time, returning friends' messages, saving for retirement, doing your taxes. They feel either a bit flat or outright aversive. If you guide your behavior by this anticipatory feeling, you will put off almost anything that might improve your outlook.

The things that we feel tempted to do are often those that make us feel worse in the long run: turn on the television, drink more, sit at home, spend impulsively, head to the casino, surf the Internet aimlessly, play computer solitaire, get into relationships or sexual encounters that you and everyone else can see are bad ideas. All you need to do is give in to temptation, and misery will knock at the door like a thirty-minute pizza delivery.

Perhaps you disagree. You can think of a few activities that you look forward to, enjoy doing, and are glad to have done: positive-positive-positive. You can also think of a few things, like compulsively hitting your thumb with a hammer, that you would dread, dislike, and regret: negative-negative-negative.

Of course. In those circumstances, it doesn't really matter whether you decide what to do based on your anticipation, enjoyment, or satisfaction—you'll make the same decision regardless. But let's be honest. There are many more things in your life that switch from positive to negative or negative to positive.

Live your life by your anticipatory feelings—your temptations—and you will often find yourself doing things that you regret and that drag you lower. You will never again pay your taxes, exercise, eat unfamiliar food, get out of bed early to go hiking, organize birthday parties for friends, or get to work on time. You will stay in your ever-shrinking comfort zone, you will indulge your worst tendencies, and you will seldom try anything new. As you place a collar around your neck and hand the leash to your temptations, they will grow in power. They will become your master, and you their slave.

After all, what's the alternative? Doing things you will be glad to have done. But that future emotion is entirely imaginary, isn't it? You'll never be certain that you are right. Maybe you'll agree to make that wedding speech and then vomit in the middle of it. Maybe you'll sign up for that 5k run and have a heart attack. Maybe you'll change the oil in the car and find an even worse problem.

Tell yourself that those who follow their future emotions are cold, passionless, overly responsible drones. Tell yourself that if you did the same, you'd have a life of mindless conformity to the standards and expectations of your culture. Ignore the fact that you would be basing your life on your *own* satisfaction, not someone else's, and that satisfaction strikes a deeper and more lasting note of enjoyment than temptation does. Tell yourself that you prefer to live by impulse, the life of a hedonist. Don't think about the fact that those others are more effective hedonists than you are.

LESSON 33

Look Out for Number One

If you ever stumble upon a poker game, it's easy to tell who is winning: it's the person sitting behind the biggest pile of chips. You should view life the same way. The winner is the one with the most elaborate house, the biggest bank account, the most expensive car, the best yacht, and the storage unit for all of the toys and treats that don't fit anywhere else.

Your objective should be to accumulate as many resources as possible. Given that accolades, money, and fame are available in finite quantities, ensure that others do not get them first. You don't hand good cards to your opponents at the poker table, so why would you do so in real life?

There are now over seven billion people on Earth, and the most important of these must be you. Be hesitant about donating your time, money, or energy to any person, group, or cause outside yourself. Remind yourself that you are not sufficiently wealthy to scatter money hither and yon, nor so idle that you can afford to stand around ladling soup to the homeless or sandbagging someone else's riverside home. To do so would imply that your own interests are not important—that *you* are not important.

At some level, deep inside, a part of you knows that you are enough and that you have enough. But if you truly believed that, what would you do? Perhaps you would begin giving it away. Money, time, energy, compassion. You might think that expending yourself for the welfare of others would ultimately help you feel impoverished again, but this tends not to work. Instead, such ill-advised generosity cultivates the part of yourself that believes in your abundance. We tend to feel wealthier by acting as though we already have more than we need.

Instead, you should jealously collect all victories, praise, and wealth to yourself. This feeds the part of us that feels impoverished and (ta dah!) makes us feel miserable.

If you live in the developed economies of the West, this cast of mind should be relatively easy to conjure and sustain. Your entire culture prepares you for it. The messages you receive help you, no matter your circumstances, to feel bereft and inferior, thus needing to focus on your own welfare before you can possibly consider anyone else's. Although this perspective may spring from the misery we seek, it also serves to perpetuate it.

The Dalai Lama has said, "If you want others to be happy, practice compassion. If you want to be happy, practice compassion." He appears to be right. One strategy for alleviating misery is to spend at least some of one's time doing things for other people. Similarly, nothing creates a sense of greater wealth and abundance than giving money away.

We might view the Dalai Lama as our rightful enemy, but flip him on his head and he becomes our ally: "If you want others to be miserable, practice indifference. If you want to be miserable, practice indifference." If you resolutely practice a lack of compassion, not only will you create unhappiness in yourself, but you will also enable others to experience it. This is the flip side of the wealth paradox: to create a sense of poverty, grasp what you have ever more tightly to your breast.

How can you stamp out compassion? One strategy is to view the misfortunes and unmet needs of others as being deserved. The poor are poor because they did not study and attend good universities, and they're simply lazy anyway. The ill clearly did not take proper care of themselves. The addicted chose to do precisely what we were all warned not to do when we were children. Victims of crime should have invested in better locks. Victims of disasters should have paid attention to the warning signs.

These people are simply experiencing the consequences of their own actions. If you act to remediate the situation, they will never learn, and others will see that they need not care for themselves because do-gooders like you will jump in and help out. If this stance seems familiar, it should: it is the prime justification for a society that demands loyalty from its citizens while doing little to improve their lives in return.

A second way to overcome any natural compassion you may harbor is to view the needs of others as a bottomless pit. No matter what you do, you can't really help anyone. Rather than taking the edge off their problems, you will only create dependence—increasing, rather than decreasing, their helplessness. Having fed the needy, their appetites will only become greater.

Finally, you can cultivate a sense of the futility of altruism by aiming high. All your life, you have watched movies in which the protagonist manages to save the world by brief and heroic action (clipping the red wire on the bomb, discovering the viral antidote, diverting the threatening asteroid). Decide that if you are going to invest your precious lifeblood in a cause, you must have the same gargantuan return. Only donate money to cancer research if it is clear that your $200 will produce the cure. Because this is manifestly unlikely, it will be easy to hold on to your time and money.

If you do get talked into helping in some way, cultivate rapid disillusionment. Point out that you spent an entire week on a housing project, and homelessness remains an issue. You sent a check for famine relief, and people are still starving. You funded your brother's rehab, and he relapsed a year later. You spoke up at the town hall meeting, but they made the wrong decision anyway.

Tell yourself that anything you can do is only a drop in the ocean. It will not change the world, and it will not be missed if you do nothing.

Ignore the impact of collective effort—how the mutual contributions of thousands combine to create great forces of change. Devalue the beneficiaries of your own contributions. So what if you funded the education of one Nepalese child—who really cares? She and her family are insignificant to you. The ego boost of a James Bond–like impact is what you were after.

To keep water in a bucket you must plug the holes. Similarly, to retain everything for yourself you must seal off your compassion. View generosity of spirit as a weakness, and stamp it out. With it will go your humanity and any happiness that would otherwise taint your misery.

LESSON 34

Duty First, Life Later

"I haven't seen a movie or read a novel since I got here."

A group of us were chatting in the hall of the psychology department, preparing for our weekly departure to the student pub. Sharon (as I'll call her) had stopped by briefly. She wouldn't be going, of course. Too busy. She was always too busy. No one was skeptical of her claim. She had never been seen at a social event in the year since our cohort started the program. She said she'd be able to relax once her master's thesis was defended.

Once that goal was accomplished, leisure continued to recede. She would relax once she had finished collecting her PhD data, once her comprehensive examinations were over, once she defended her dissertation, once she'd completed her year of postdoctoral supervision.

I haven't seen her in many years, but she's always been there in the back of my mind. I've wondered if she's still at it. *Once I've published some articles. Once I've gotten a promotion. Once my private practice is running. Once the mortgage is paid off. Once I retire. Then my life will start. Unless something else gets in the way.*

The Marshmallow Test is an assessment of a child's ability to delay gratification. The experimenter presents the child with a marshmallow and announces that she will be back in fifteen minutes. If the marshmallow hasn't been eaten at that point, the child can have a second one.

Children vary in their ability to sit in front of the marshmallow and not eat it. Some give in immediately, while others squirm in agonies of temptation. It turns out that the simple binary outcome (eaten or not) is nicely predictive of later academic success. Delayers generally do better. It's easy to see why. Success depends to a great extent on a person's ability to study when they could be watching television and to work their way through the boring bits of otherwise interesting projects.

Adults sometimes respond to a description of the test with a sigh of ennui. "I don't like marshmallows anyway, so I don't see the relevance." Swap out the marshmallow with the grown-up equivalent, however, and watch the fun. Lift the cover and reveal a plate of chocolate. A line of cocaine. A bottle of scotch. A pornographic video. A television remote. A couch. Suddenly the test isn't quite so hypothetical. Leave them for fifteen minutes, and only the crumbs remain.

The ability to delay gratification is a double-edged sword, with misery lying seductively on both sides. Too little self-discipline, and we accomplish nothing, wallowing in our consumption. Too much, and we can choke the joy out of our lives. It is only along the narrow flat of the blade that happiness-inducing moderation can be found. This tightrope is easily avoided. If you become especially adept at passing the Marshmallow Test, you may suppress even your better aspirations in favor of conformity to the expectations or wishes of others. You may also become so focused on a single, genuinely held goal (like becoming a respected professional) that your life becomes imbalanced. You may spend no time socializing with friends, enjoying life, or doing any of the things that sustain you for the long haul. Even if you can keep the flame of your passion burning, you may find that you have realized one life goal (such as career success) but missed out on all the others.

You can choose to push most of your goals or pleasures into the future, telling yourself that there will always be time for them later. Relationships, novels, travel, experiences, contributions to the world. Dinner with friends. Playing with the cat. Walking in the forest. Even a night at the pub. It may turn out that the future is shorter than you thought it would be. And when "later" appears, if it ever does, you may have forgotten what your plans were, or what your life was meant to be about. You will no longer know how to have fun, how to lie in a hammock, how to be a friend, how to raise your children. You will only remember how to be working, working, working.

Sharon would have passed the Marshmallow Test with no difficulty. I think I would have too—as a child, I still had uneaten Halloween candy in January. But I had the example of a father who delayed gratification constantly, apparently believing that he would start living his life when he retired—something he died before doing. So in graduate school I went to the pub, I saw movies, I read books, and I had relationships. I lived my life, knowing that the future was an imaginary construct that might not exist.

Don't use me as your model: I wasn't trying to be unhappy. That, when it happened, was accidental. Instead, use Sharon. If you have a sense of what you would like your life to be about, set that insight aside. Tell yourself that you have more important things to think about right now—like completing your degree or getting your career established or paying off the mortgage. Right now you have to work hard. You are sacrificing for a distant future. If the present does not seem very enjoyable, that's all right. The future will be all the rosier for it.

Tell yourself that when you just reach that next hurdle, you'll be able to sit back, relax, and work on your life's purpose. There's plenty of time. You can get to it when your to-do list runs out. Become a supreme delayer of gratification. Push your life endlessly into the future. Forget balance. Hang on to the marshmallow long enough, and it will become inedible.

It's important to suppress any awareness of the tendency to fix your eyes on a new hurdle when you pass the previous one. Just keep going, task after task, until the sand in the hourglass runs out—or until it has been so long since you considered what you really wanted that you can no longer remember what it was.

Live the Unlived Lives of Others

"I don't think I ever wanted to be a lawyer."

This sentence, and others much like it, is uttered in psychologists' consulting rooms with surprising regularity. One of the prime motivators for people entering psychotherapy is a sense of diminishing enthusiasm about their lives—a feeling that, though they have continued to consume the same diet, its ability to nourish and energize them has withered away.

This fading of energy and enthusiasm is often seen in people at midlife. They spend their early adulthoods beavering away, getting little emotional return from their lives, in the belief that they are building for a bright and shiny future. In early middle age they realize that they can no longer convince themselves that they are sacrificing for an eventual prize. They have arrived at the future, and it is not nearly as fulfilling as they anticipated. If the payoff has not yet come, perhaps it never will.

How did they manage to take what appears to have been a blind alley? This book, after all, is about the pursuit of dead ends and the real estate to be found there.

Fritz Perls, famed developer of Gestalt therapy, believed that many people find themselves in a life created from a mixture of adolescent interests and the expectations of others (parents, teachers, mentors). Initially somewhat fluid, their lives harden into concrete, and they find themselves trapped in an existence that does not suit them.

Jungian analyst James Hollis seems to agree. In *The Middle Passage*, his excellent book on midlife, Hollis suggests that we start our lives learning how to be children and, just as we get accomplished at it, the rules change and we are expected to behave like adults. Not knowing how to do this, we look around and build our adult selves from the examples and pressures around us rather than from our inherent interests and talents. At first this seems to work: we achieve some successes and create a passable facsimile of maturity. Eventually, though, our true nature comes back to haunt us, demanding to be heard.

Hollis and others suggest that the source of much misery is the unconscious impulse to fulfill the incomplete life mission of one's parents. Dad always wanted to be a lawyer, so we became one. Mom never achieved her dream of stardom, so we tap-danced our way onto the stage with her pushing us forward.

Whether incomplete or not, there can be a powerful desire to fill the shoes your parents made for you. They had a child, after all, because they had an image of the adult you would become. Become it.

Whether your mission is to climb upward or rappel downward in your life, it can be useful to examine the core motivations of your parents and other significant figures from your formative years. What were their goals—and which of these were thwarted or left incomplete? Out of your caring for them, or your wish to please, or your outright guilt at the opportunities you have been given, you may experience an impulse to take up their torch and live out their lives rather than your own.

If you would like to live your own life instead, treat with suspicion the concordances between your present life and the unlived lives of your predecessors. Is it simply a welcome coincidence that your true desires match up so nicely with theirs, or have you subjugated your own interests to live someone else's life?

If you are on board with the aims of this book, however, you can use these indicators as beacons to the unsatisfying life. Tell yourself how pleased your mother would be if you married a wealthy man, which she always wished she had done. Remind yourself of the plans of your deceased brother, and set aside your own life to fulfill his. Know that your parents always expected to have a heterosexual son and grandchildren, so devote your life to creating that illusion for them.

To be unhappy, set out on someone else's life path. It will prove difficult at first, but it will become easier with time. Eventually your own impulses and aspirations will begin to fade. You will have been on that road long enough that your own existence will have dropped beneath the horizon behind you. With it will have gone your vitality, your enthusiasm, and your motivation. Your misery will remain, like the flecks of precious gold in a miner's pan.

Stay in Your Zone of Comfort

"If it hurts to do that, then don't do it." The logic is unassailable. If you are afraid of dogs, stay away from dogs. *Et voila!* The problem is solved. The only question is: does this strategy point the way toward happiness or misery?

Answer: both. Short-term happiness and long-term misery. In this book we are not striving for the cheap, momentary mood dip. We want full, resilient, lasting darkness, so an initial flicker of relief is nothing to worry about.

Divide your life into two realms. First, the Zone of Comfort. This consists of places, roles, situations, and activities that feel familiar and relatively stress-free. Staying at home watching your favorite game show on television. Taking the same route to the same mall to shop at the same stores. Working at the same, comfortable job, doing the same tasks the same way you have always done them. Visiting the same restaurant and ordering the same thing. Returning to the same vacation spot you've visited a dozen times before. Helping out in the background at your nephew's wedding.

The second realm is the Zone of Discomfort. This is different for everyone. Turning off the television and going to the concert in the park by the band you're not sure you like. Taking an unfamiliar route (or public transit) to a part of the city you've never visited. At work, trying out new ways of doing old tasks and volunteering for projects you haven't done before. Finding a new restaurant and ordering something you've never had. Vacationing somewhere you've never been and doing things differently (like cycling, camping, or staying in hostels). Volunteering to give a toast at your nephew's wedding.

Residing within your Zone of Comfort is warm, reassuring, and very tempting. But when you wake up one day from a nap, you will notice that your bookcase has shifted. This familiar room is shrinking, millimeter by millimeter. Once, you felt fine visiting all but the busiest malls. Today you can detect a flutter of anxiety in a convenience store. Once, your avoidance of crowds was a subtle preference; now it is an overwhelming need. Once, the thought of speaking up in a meeting was mildly concerning; now it provokes outright panic. The Zone of Comfort hides a secret: the longer you spend in it, the smaller it gets.

Venture into the Zone of Discomfort, and it too changes. Drive the unfamiliar route three times, and it ceases to seem strange. The boundaries redraw themselves, and what was once threatening becomes easier. The Zone of Discomfort shrinks when you enter it. The Zone of Comfort grows only by leaving it.

To become less happy, then, simply obey your impulses. They will almost always point to the activity you've tried before, to the easier option, to staying home rather than leaving familiar walls behind. A part of your brain, monitoring your behavior, will conclude that the paths you have not taken must truly be unwise and threatening, and your inward impulse will become steadily stronger. What seemed like a momentary preference will become an urgent need for safety and familiarity.

So listen to your fears and take them seriously. Avoid dogs, heights, crowds, enclosed spaces, travel, public speaking, romantic entanglements, airplanes, tests of your ability, medical appointments, job interviews, and all potential humiliations. Announce that you will be perfectly happy to dive into the pool as soon as you feel comfortable with the water. Then settle back in your easy chair and wait for the necessary confidence to arrive. It never will. And you will maintain a smaller life forever.

It is better still, of course, if your Zone of Comfort is small to begin with. Therapists around the world have noticed the emergence of a cohort of young people (mostly males, for reasons that remain obscure) who, socially anxious and unwilling to challenge their fears, never take flight and leave their parents' homes. We have created a world where such a life is possible and, at least for them, tolerable. They have the Internet, they have video games, and often they have parents willing to serve as household staff and fund the retreat.

These "lost boys" (as they are sometimes called) spend their lives in basement rooms, waiting for their self-assurance to arrive. They have been told—often by the educational system—that without unshakeable confidence and flawless self-esteem, they can no more leave home than they would without clothes. So they sit listening for the doorbell, waiting in vain for their delivery.

No one has told them, it seems, that confidence does not precede action; it follows. We feel comfortable in the water only once we have been paddling awhile. The ungrounded, uncertain feeling is what we get when we leave the Zone of Comfort to do something new. It is not a signal to retreat; it is the sensation of one's life expanding.

It is not too late to emulate the lost boys, no matter what your position in life might be. Simply turn down all challenges. Use your discomfort as your guide. Ignore all exhortations to *make your fears your agenda.* This is for people wishing a larger life, not a smaller one.

The meaning of your shrinking life should be to create comfort and calm and to avoid stress, preferably twenty-four hours a day. The term for this strategy is *lining one's coffin.* Rather than engaging in real life, with all of its messy emotions, conflicts, and disappointments, retreat into comfort. When your life knocks at the door, turn off the lights and hide behind the fridge as though you're avoiding an unwelcome religious representative.

You'll feel better. For a while, anyway.

LESSON 37

Avoid Solitude

"I know, let's split up." It's the groaner moment in almost every horror film. The zombies, the vampires, the aliens are everywhere, and for the moment our heroes are reasonably safe. But they have to find the book, the exit, the crucifix, the spell, the silver bullets, the light switch. The obvious thing to do? Go off by themselves so they can be picked off one by one. You would never do this. Never.

Time for another in a series of Catch-22s. In the preceding chapter, we discussed isolation as a misery-inducing strategy. Here's another route downward: avoid solitude at all costs.

Treat your entire life as though you were in one of those horror films, but refuse to make the classic mistake. Instead, obsessively surround yourself with people every moment. Create plans for every day, every evening, every weekend. Then create backup plans in case people cancel out. Then create backups for the backups.

Do this not because you love and enjoy these people so much. In fact, this strategy works best if you feel no strong attachment to the people with whom you spend time. Instead, do it to avoid the horrifying prospect of being alone. Treat solitude as a threat, a vulnerable time in which the villain can attack.

Who is this dire enemy, you might well wonder. Why, it's you, of course. Your own mind. If you spend an evening alone, your mind will start whispering to you. *You are alone. You are unloved. You have no friends. You never did. You never will. You are worthless. You do not even exist, really. A room with only you in it is an empty space.*

Sitting alone and listening to this chilling voice sounds like an excellent misery-inducing strategy, so how might avoiding it lead downhill?

Easy. No matter how many social engagements you arrange, you will never entirely convince yourself that you are worthwhile or loved. Think how much effort it takes to book up your schedule. Others, surely, don't have to dig so deep. Your friends invite you less often than you invite them. Maybe they only agree to your suggestions because they just don't know how to say no.

Also, the urgent effort to avoid solitude will only convince your unconscious mind of the hazards of being alone. Like a person who runs screaming from a spider, your avoidance only serves to reinforce the fear. Rather than social contact being a preference, it will become a life-or-death need. You may sigh with relief that this week you have escaped being left alone, but will you manage it next week or the week after?

If you self-impose occasional solitary evenings or weekends, eventually you will rob them of their fearfulness. Having survived again and again, you will begin to see solitude as survivable—and perhaps even attractive. You will learn that you can read alone, do chores alone, exercise alone, see movies alone, eat in restaurants alone, pursue your interests alone, and nothing terrible happens. You may also discover that creativity, personal exploration, and learning are often best accomplished solo—that certain steps forward are only possible when you are not distracted by social contact.

Could there be an opportunity for unhappiness here? Perhaps, having learned that you do not need people every minute, you will become a hermit and spiral into misery that way. Alas, this is unlikely. By cherishing solitary time, a thirst for social contact will usually develop, making companionship even more welcome and enjoyable. The frantic avoidance of solitude is a more certain path downward.

So get out your calendar and book it up. Leave yourself no time for reflection or recharging. Should you accidentally find yourself with nothing to do, turn on the computer. When social life is lacking, social media can pick up the slack. Skate from site to site, using Facebook and Skype and Twitter as putty to fill the gaps. And if that becomes too tedious? Hey: avoiding solitude is what television is for.

LESSON 38

Choose Fashion over Style

Quentin Crisp was a flamboyantly gay Englishman employed for much of his life as a model for government art schools in Britain—a profession that provided the title of his autobiography and the subsequent John Hurt film, *The Naked Civil Servant*. He survived the Blitz and the distinctly disapproving social environment of midcentury London, and at seventy-two he abruptly moved to New York City, where he knew next to no one.

Over the next eighteen years he became a fixture of the city, appearing repeatedly on *Late Night with David Letterman*, performing on stage (especially in his one-man show, *An Evening with Quentin Crisp*) and in films (appearing, for example, as Elizabeth I in *Orlando*), and writing a dozen books about his life and philosophy. He is the subject of a well-known song by Sting ("An Englishman in New York"). He died in 1999 at the age of ninety, about to open a run of his show in his native England.

Beneath the henna, ascots, and makeup was a remarkably incisive intellect and a powerfully independent man. In books such as *How to Have a Lifestyle*, Crisp outlined his philosophy of self-determination. One of his pet concerns was the nature of style.

Most people view the words *fashion* and *style* as near-synonyms. Crisp insisted that they were opposites. He felt that one of the driving motivations of most humans is the desire to eliminate their own uniqueness—a kind of psychological suicide that Freud might have likened to Thanatos, the death instinct.

Fashion, in Crisp's view, is the art of denying one's individuality in order to adopt the uniforms and dictates of culture, as determined by people who

1. have never met you, and

2. do not care whether you exist.

The implicit goal is to cover your imperfections and become something you are not: a person who is acceptable in the eyes of others. A pleasing shell with no discernible interior. In Crisp's words, "Fashion is what you adopt when you don't know who you are."

Style, on the other hand, is the art of bringing your defining individual features to the fore, regardless of what others might expect or find acceptable:

- If you are tall, he felt you should let yourself be tall. Do not stoop, do not shrink yourself, do not try to fit in with a smaller world.

- If you are short, be short—never wear heels.

- If you have an opinion, express it; an interest, follow it.

In brief, be who you are. Make no attempt to fit in.

Crisp saw this as a purposeful and conscious act of personal development. Unlike many, he did not believe that being yourself is simply a matter of self-expression—a loosening of your own leash or a random pushing outward of everything inside. When we appeared on this planet, our only means of self-expression was to look around, cry, and create puddles. Everything else came later.

In his view, becoming who you are is a lifelong and very deliberate act of personal self-creation. It is an art form. If you want to be a multilingual conversationalist, this won't happen on its own. You have to enroll in some language courses and cultivate your knowledge base. In a sense, the life we choose to lead creates us. He points out, "It's no good running a pig farm for thirty years while saying, 'Really, I was meant to be a ballet dancer.' By then, pigs will be your style."

The trick, of course, is figuring out the elements of one's personal style. In psychotherapy, we often employ questions as sharp paring knives to get to the core of life's issues. Crisp proposed a particularly potent question best avoided by seekers of the dark side of emotional life: "If there were no applause and no criticism, who would you be?"

If, in other words, nothing you do can impress anyone, and nothing could attract their disapproval, what would you do? In this imaginary world of social equanimity, what might govern your behavior? Your motivation would have to come from within and be directed by your own interests.

Once you've figured out what you would do on his imaginary planet, Crisp doesn't order you to act automatically on your insight as though you really lived there. His question is designed to clarify your options, not narrow them. The truth is, we do live in a world of applause and criticism, and at least some of our behavior will always be governed by the hope and fear they create.

For our purposes, Crisp's flashlight illuminates the reverse path as effectively as the route to selfhood. If the road northward involves choosing style over fashion, then those of us who want our lives to go south should choose fashion over style.

So listen to the recommendations of cultural gurus and follow instructions. Base your life on the pursuit of the admiration and approval of others. Take out a nail file and scrape away any of your troubling uniqueness. Regard your personal talents, quirks, and interests as impediments to the real goal, which is to camouflage yourself, like a chameleon, in your surroundings.

Even more importantly, determine which aspects of your nature might attract the disapproval of others. Hide these away. This will enable you to starve those parts of yourself and to feel shame for their very existence. Remind yourself that if people saw the real you, they would reject you. This will disqualify any approval you receive as having been obtained under false pretenses.

In sum, ask yourself the question of the Anti-Crisp. "If the applause and criticism of others was your only guide, who would you be?"

Look for the herd. They must be galloping off in that chosen direction for a reason. Follow them and attempt to vanish in their midst.

Pursue Happiness Relentlessly

Happiness is suddenly all the rage. Workshops, online courses, scientific research. Books on the subject climb the bestseller lists. Even the volume you presently hold can be (mis)construed as a backhanded stab at happiness. The successful pursuer, it is implied, will be happy twenty-four hours a day.

What has this got to do with misery? It turns out that the relentless pursuit of happiness is actually a fairly good way of producing its opposite. There are three primary reasons for this: Utility, expectancy, and interpretation. Let's consider these in order.

First, utility. Imagine an airplane cockpit. There are multiple dials and indicators: the altimeter, compass, fuel gauge, airspeed indicator, and so on. Each has a purpose. Now imagine a pilot who offers to take you for a spin. You look at the controls and see that most of them have been taped over. "I don't really like the compass, it makes me feel restricted," he explains. "Or the fuel gauge, it just makes me anxious. I only like the airspeed indicator. I like to go fast."

Do you fly with him?

You would probably be tempted to point out that all of the gauges have important information to provide, whether the news is good or not.

Like the controls of a plane, the emotions operate as a kind of behavioral guidance system, letting us know about the environment, dangers ahead, and the impacts of our actions:

- Anger informs us that someone may be impinging on our boundaries.

- Fear alerts us to threats.

- Guilt lets us know that we have violated our own standards.

- Happiness says, "Whatever you just did was great, do it again."

Most of us need all the advice we can get. A guidance system that can only say, "Go left, go left, go left" is limited in its usefulness. We will ignore threats, miss cues, never defend ourselves, and behave badly—smiling in the short term but bringing disaster down on our heads. In the same way that eliminating most cockpit gauges leads to unhappy flights, then, ignoring negative emotions will tend to magnify our misery.

What about expectancy? Let's do another thought experiment. Imagine that a friend sees a discarded lottery ticket on your table and says, "I follow this lottery—I think you've won $10." You go to the local shop, and the attendant informs you that you have actually won $10,000. How do you feel?

Try it again. Your friend sees the lottery ticket and says, "I think you've won $10 million." The shopkeeper confirms the win, but it is actually $10,000. How do you feel?

If you are like most people, your reactions in the two situations are quite different: pleasure in the first and disappointment in the second. But the actual situation—winning $10,000—is the same. The difference is accounted for by your expectations as you run to the shop. The higher you set your expectations, the more disappointment you feel.

So it is with the quest for happiness. If you believe that you can be unfailingly, unremittingly happy all of the time, reality will smack you in the face with the fact that you are simply not wired for constant good cheer. The disappointment will, instead, propel your mood in the opposite direction. As Edward de Bono once said, "Unhappiness is best defined as the difference between our talents and our expectations." For maximum misery, then, set your expectations high.

The third misery-inducing aspect of the quest for happiness involves interpretation. Cognitive therapists argue that most of our emotions arise from our appraisals of events, not from the events themselves. The frown on our partner's face is not so alarming; it is what we think the frown means that bothers us.

Traditional cognitive therapy emphasizes our evaluations of external events (such as receiving an ominous envelope from the tax department or noticing that our youngest child is late coming home from her first date). But we also appraise our own reactions, emotions, and behavior. If we see uncomfortable emotions as normal parts of life, as indeed they are, we will experience sadness or anxiety and accept them and the guidance they may give us.

If we strive for constant happiness, however, we will inevitably change the interpretations that we make when another selection emerges from the emotional vending machine. We have failed. This is not a normal part of life; it is a sign of our own faultiness. Many of our most intense miseries arise from the exaggerated meanings we assign to our own internal experiences:

- "My jealousy is childish."

- "That panic attack means that I am weak."

- "My sadness is a sign of the futility of all my efforts."

In order to increase misery, then, view happiness as the only normal state, and your uncomfortable emotions as reflections upon you. Make them deeply meaningful. They prove that you are, as you have long suspected, flawed and inferior.

Does all of this mean that the whole happiness industry is really just a sham? Not entirely. Those wishing to become at least somewhat happier can do so, paradoxically, by giving up their laser-focus on the quest. Happiness is incidental—a result of doing something else, pursuing some other goal, or being involved in some other activity. Pursuing happiness is like chasing squirrels: you will never overtake your quarry. To get close to a squirrel, you must arrange yourself so the squirrel will come to you. To increase happiness, you must arrange your mind or your life so happiness appears as a natural consequence.

One strategy for bringing about life dissatisfaction, then, is to ignore the role of meaning in your life. Another is to elevate the pursuit of happiness to the throne and make it your sole aim. Happiness is the outcome, not the path; it is the result of producing meaning in one's life, not the meaning itself.

Improve Yourself

Perhaps you found this book in the self-help section of your local bookstore. If so, there were thousands of other books there too. Go back and buy them. Tell yourself that your real agenda, whether or not you go along with the downward trajectory described by this book, is to become a better person.

Occupy yourself entirely with the arduous task of erasing your flaws. Read only self-help literature, never anything else. When you take a course, make it one about personal development. When you watch television, switch to the shows about overcoming addiction, losing weight, getting in shape, or finding your true self.

Make the overcoming of your imperfections the overriding goal of your life. Tell yourself that you will stop once you are eighty pounds lighter. Once you have fully processed your childhood traumas. Once you have six-pack abs. Once you sit in the corner office. Once your marriage is seamlessly joyful. Once you can say that every day, and in every way, you are getting better and better.

Stop, in other words, only when you are finally *good enough*: when you have crossed that shining threshold and have become acceptable—in your own eyes and in the eyes of everyone else. The ads, the book covers, the workshop posters—they all have pictures of these people. The flawless ones. The smiling ones with the white teeth and perfect hair. You could be one of them. Tell yourself that.

A friend of a friend once commented to me that he was en route to the chiropractor and that later that day, he had his therapy appointment. I said that I didn't know that he was having trouble. He wasn't; he told me: "Maintenance." His maintenance consisted of a dozen separate appointments through the week. They kept him aloft. And in misery-inducing debt.

You have almost certainly wondered for most of your life if you were ever going to become one of those radiant, successful people on the book covers. Here's where you find out, because I'm going to tell you.

No. You're not.

Sorry.

The problem is that your culture doesn't just demand tangle-free hair. It has a whole list of criteria. You have to be smart enough, informed enough, fit enough, thin enough, rich enough, wise enough, happy enough, sexy enough, popular enough, and stable enough. You must not have panic attacks, bad breath, sad mornings, hangovers, loneliness, crow's feet, high cholesterol, debt, clutter, a straying spouse, spiritual uncertainty, shyness, a sweet tooth, thinning hair, a thickening waist, wrinkles, depression, disability, career angst, bad spelling, or body odor.

Even if you manage to meet some of these criteria, you will never—*never*—reach all of them, no matter how long you live. You will never be a success by the full standards of your culture. If you must be good enough by those standards in order to relax and enjoy your life, then that dream will never come to pass. Sell the hammock; you will never be able to relax in it.

In part, this troubling reality exists because it is not in the best interests of our culture for you to feel good about yourself. The economy needs to sell you products, so it needs you to see yourself as lacking. But in part, the futility of the task arises from the unbounded optimism of personal development. We can all be highly effective persons; we can all find success in ten days or less; we can all be the best we can be; we can all discover the creative genius within; we can all be president.

So keep trying. Tell yourself that you are not good enough. Find ever more areas where you are faulty and shameful. Spend your life trying to manifest excellence in your life. The hidden observer at the back of your mind will watch you. It will see the intensity of your efforts and conclude that to work so hard you must truly be as deficient as you imagine. Maybe worse.

There is one question you must never ask yourself. "If I were already good enough, what would I do then?"

If, that is, you didn't have to make up for your inadequacy, what would you do with your life? If you did not have to paper over your faults, what would you read? What films would you see? What courses would you take? Where would you go? Having become fully capable, what would you use that capacity for? Where would you make your contribution?

If you ask questions like these, all your work on the misery project might come undone. You might begin living your life, rather than preparing for it, and you might discover that that alone can sustain you, elevate your mood, and destroy the cynicism and unhappiness you have worked so hard to create.

So go back to the bookstore. Did all those books about how to become good enough seem aimed in a happier direction than this one? Not at all. Get into therapy. Better yet, get into three different kinds at once. Focus on becoming what no one, not even the models in those photographs, can be: good enough. On all levels.

It's not a pot of gold at the end of the rainbow, after all. It's you.

Chase it.

Ending the Misery Project: Life on the Top Floor

Human misery must somewhere have a stop; there is no wind that always blows a storm.

—Euripides

The window of my office looks out on Vancouver General Hospital, where the main tower rises over the city. It has a stepped profile, providing terraces on several of the upper floors. When the tower was built, the top floor was originally planned to be for the administration. The president of the hospital would look out over the campus from sixteen floors up.

The hospital staff rebelled. They knew what they wanted on the top floor, and they won. Palliative Care. Today, this is where patients go when the time for active treatment is over. It's easy to imagine that it would be a desperately sad and pain-filled place. For the most part, though, it isn't. There are kitchens and lounges, an extensive rooftop garden, and an air of relaxed calm.

The primary agenda is comfort, contemplation, and preparation for the closing moments of a life.

The tower sits on the upper edge of a slope that leads down to the waters of an inlet. It is the tallest structure in that area. From Palliative Care, patients and their visitors get one of the longest, widest, most unobstructed views in the city.

This is appropriate. It is a place to take the long view.

I've spent a lot of time there. With family, with a friend whose brain tumor resisted all treatment, and with patients.

It's true what they say. No one wishes that they'd spent more time at the office. Nor that they'd accumulated more toys. Nor that the lawn was weed-free.

Typically they look back with a mixture of satisfaction and bewilderment. Satisfaction: time spent with friends and family. Contributions made. Experiences lived.

And bewilderment: "What was I doing? Why did I think those things were so important that I spent most of my life on them?" Overwork. Television. Striving for promotions. Obsessing over the news. Worrying what others might think. Putting off life, putting off life, putting off life.

Until now. Here. Where there is only one task. To be here. Be present. Until they can't be here anymore.

It is as though you have spent your life trying to discern something that sits mysteriously behind a curtain, and when you arrive at the top floor, they lift the curtain and show you what was there all along. You don't have to wait for whatever comes after your last breath to find out the meaning of the story. You find out there, in that bed. It was people. It was friendship. It was connection. It was becoming who you really are. It was the experience, the full experience, of life itself.

Generally the inhabitants of the top floor have journeyed beyond distant desires. But there is a wistfulness, a wish that they could go back in time and try the whole thing again, with the curtain raised this time. They can't, but they could teach.

It's a shame, in a way, that the ward is way up there. Maybe it should be in the hospital's lobby, where people could stop by and be reminded. Maybe it should be at an intersection, in a big-box store, on a subway platform. They would look out calmly from their beds and gaze at us. Remember. Remember. You'll be here sooner than you think.

THE CAUSES OF MISERY

Sit in a therapist's chair for a while. Thirty years, perhaps. Keep a notepad by your side, and list the ways that life can go suddenly, unexpectedly, uncontrollably wrong. It will be a long list and, just when you think you have heard every conceivable form of tragedy and misfortune, someone sits down and gives you four more. Life is difficult and unpredictable. Much of our personal unhappiness will arise from events over which we have little control. This list is what, in the introduction to this little book, we decided to call "Column A."

It is tempting to believe that even our day-to-day unhappiness is of this sort. Things happen, and we react. There's nothing we can do. But if we look carefully, we see that there is also a Column B. These are the downward influences that are at least partially under our own control; the product of our own choices and actions. Hostilities expressed. Flawed impulses obeyed. Addictions fed. Avoidance indulged.

Add Column B to Column A, and you have the weight that we carry on our shoulders. We'd like to believe that it is entirely Column A that weighs us down, and at times, it is. But for most of us, most of the time, Column B contributes just as much. Especially when we add the influence of our thinking: the things we ruminate over, the people we take for granted, the stories about our misfortune that we create in our minds.

We will never shrug off all of that weight. But we can realize that at least some of it is optional.

AND NOW, LADIES AND GENTLEMEN, PLEASE REMOVE YOUR MASKS

All right. Here's the wink at last.

You and I both know that you don't really aspire to the goals set out in this book. You've explored the valleys enough. You're looking for the mountaintops instead. So what have we been doing here?

We spend our lives stumbling through the underbrush, trying to find the path to fulfillment, contentment, or, yes, happiness. Most of the time, we know we're not on the trail, but it's devilishly hard to see with any clarity. Now and then, it can be useful to turn around and look in the other direction. By doing so, we can notice the general angle of the route, and we can see how much of the time we have been walking downward instead of up.

In our post-hospitalization depression groups, clients were asked to contemplate what they would do if they wanted to feel worse. This was not a goal any of them truly held. They were desperate to feel better. Just like us, much of the time. They were routinely surprised that the menu of strategies to darken their lives often summed up their daily schedule. It's tempting to strike one's forehead or curse perverse human nature at this realization—or to suspect that evil forces within secretly want us to be miserable.

They don't. The suite of emotions with which we are equipped try to steer us away from the painful and toward the pleasurable. As far as psychology has been able to determine, we have no instinct toward self-destruction or misery—regardless of what Freud, depression statistics, or the grim nightly news might have to say about it.

So why do we find ourselves behaving so often in a manner that any sane observer could tell us will make us feel worse? There are many factors at play. Let's just consider four of them.

SHORT TERM, LONG TERM

Much of the problem lies in the fact that many acts (eating a bowl of chocolate-covered coffee beans, snapping at one's spouse, neglecting to return to work after lunch) have both positive and negative elements that shift over time. We cannot choose a course of action simply because "it makes me feel good." The same act makes us feel both good and bad at different moments.

Avoiding the walk over a high bridge satisfies the phobic's desire not to feel anxiety, but doing so repeatedly tends to reinforce and magnify the fear. Having another drink enhances the experience of the raucous bar but detracts from the pleasure of the following day. The chocolate-covered beans are nice on the tongue, but eating too many of them induces unpleasant anxiety.

Emotional pain, then, often arises when we choose the immediate pleasure over the long-term (and longer-lasting) discomfort that will result. We give ourselves a little boost followed by a deeper dip, then recover by giving ourselves another little boost, and we take another step downward. We pluck roses all along the road into misery, never realizing where we are headed.

PAIN-BASED IMPULSES

We often think of sadness as an end state—the result of painful experiences or of our own poor judgment. But emotion itself feeds back and influences thought and behavior. When we are feeling low, our motivational matrix shifts dramatically. Our horizon shortens, tempting us to act based on short-term outcomes more than we usually would. "I don't care! I just need to survive the morning."

But the options that seem attractive can morph as well. Ordinarily, a densely packed and unfailingly social restaurant might draw us in. When we are sad or depressed, however, we will feel drawn to our own home, where we can simply thaw out some leftovers and be left in peace. Normally the prospect of a run by the ocean might seem idyllic. When we are overtaken with ennui, such a pursuit may only seem pointless and tiring. The resulting choices—inactivity, isolation, procrastination— often serve only to magnify the intensity of the negative state.

This phenomenon can be so pronounced that I offer it as a general principle to client suffering from misery. *When you are feeling down, the majority of temptations you experience will lead you even lower.*

It is as though our emotions mutiny and jump ship, switching their allegiance to our worst enemy: despair. By following the siren song of their exhortations ("Call in sick and close the curtains, you'll feel better!"), we will only erode our mood further.

Instead, when our mood darkens we need to treat our instincts with suspicion. Usually we will experience relief only when we learn to act against our temptations, often engaging in what psychologist Marsha Linehan (developer of dialectical behavior therapy) calls Opposite Action. We feel tempted to withdraw, and so we approach instead. We feel exhausted, but we use this as our cue to get more exercise. Itching to defend ourselves by attacking others, we instead cultivate compassion. Agitated and antsy, we take ten minutes to sit quietly and meditate.

We notice the impulse, know that it leads downward, and turn right rather than left.

AN UNRELIABLE CRYSTAL BALL

As discussed earlier in this book, psychologist Daniel Gilbert has summarized the literature indicating that humans are remarkably poor at predicting how future actions will affect mood. Basing much or most of our behavior on these predictions, we all too frequently find ourselves worse off than when we began. We sacrifice time with loved ones to pursue ever-larger heaps of money; we liquidate our savings to buy unsatisfying toys; we gamble our marriage on the momentary excitements of an affair.

But what other option do we have? Our predictive abilities may be poor, but surely we have to base our decisions on something. If not on our clouded vision of the future, then on what?

Perhaps the past has much to teach us. Relatively few of our decisions are about entirely novel realms of activity. We can look back over our shoulder at how things have gone for us in similar situations previously. Although a three-week golfing vacation sounds lovely to our overworked self, we can remember past occasions when, after three days of golf, we were bored to tears.

When tempted by the aroma of coffee in the evening, we can recall past sleepless hyper-caffeinated nights. While experiencing the longing for a new vehicle, we can remind ourselves how short-lived the high of purchasing the last one was. Admiring the lusty twinkle in the eye of the bike gang member, we can remind ourselves of how previous experiences with such men have turned out.

Experience, as they say, can be a great teacher. But only if it is invited into the room and asked what it knows. It dresses dowdily, however, and often seems a bit too sober and dull. Not nearly as sexy or exciting as the scantily clad future, which beckons to us with such promise. Learning from experience—one of the prime pillars of wisdom—means turning away from our illusions and taking a clear-eyed look at the past.

A CULTURE WITH AN AGENDA

While we are contemplating how to arrange a happy and contented future for ourselves, we sit surrounded by our culture. The culture makes suggestions and threatens us with expulsion if we do not obey. Indeed, one way of defining a culture is by its set of ideas about how to live or have a good life. We have no shortage of advice on the matter. It can be instructive to spend an entire day listening intently for the messages the culture gives us about how to be happier—and then to analyze each one to see whether it is accurate.

One of the main problems we face is that, although many of our culture's messages are framed as ways to enhance our lives, very few of them are actually designed with that outcome in mind. Messages are formulated and delivered with other intentions. Chief among these is the aim of selling products of various kinds. If you buy this dish soap, you will be as cheerful as the househusband in the advertisement. If you watch this television news program (and its commercials) you will be better informed about the world. If you vote for this candidate, a virtual paradise on Earth will be founded, and corruption will forevermore be a thing of the past.

Messages from other sources tempt us with insider knowledge that will make us part of a select group. Adopt these beliefs, and your place in the afterlife will be assured. Learn about various conspiracies, and the veils of illusion will fall from your eyes. Simultaneously, the conversion of another acolyte will serve to reassure your informants that they themselves are on the right track and not, after all, deluded.

Messages from our own social tribes, while typically well intentioned, may simultaneously have the agenda of shaping our behavior to suit other needs—whether or not this is intended or realized by those delivering them. If we go into law, we may satisfy our father's long-held but never-realized ambition to be a lawyer. If we lose weight, we may help our cousin put to rest her suspicion that her own obsession with appearance is unhealthy. If we conform socially, physically, and professionally, we can reassure our peers that they have made the right decisions—and compromises—in their own lives.

The result is that the messages we hear almost always have a dual intent. The surface message is usually "Here's how to be happier," but the hidden and hard-to-discern intent skews the message. Unless we are able to divine and evaluate the alternative motives, the message itself may take us in the wrong direction.

For all of these reasons, we frequently find ourselves walking the trail from misery to fulfillment, but in the wrong direction. We can attribute this to our self-destructiveness, or to the death instinct, or to secondary gain, or simply to being stupid. But these explanations are generally untrue and serve only to obscure the real forces that lead us astray.

Far better than insulting ourselves or forcing ourselves to feel guilty or foolish is to adopt a posture of detached interest. Rather than panicking, we can simply sit back and notice, calmly, that we are once again in a position of deep emotional discomfort. It has visited us before, this feeling. The very fact that we recognize it tells us that we survived it the last time it stopped by. This means we are most likely to survive it this time as well. No need to fear it. Just as we might notice that our keys are missing and calmly retrace our steps since we last saw them, we can think back and see whether any of our own actions or ways of thinking may have helped bring us to this unwelcome destination.

One of the best strategies for cultivating this ability is to do just what you have been doing as you have been reading this book. Imagine that, for some perverse reason, you wanted to feel worse, not better. What would you do? What have you done in the past? How effective has that been at lowering your mood?

One of my earliest therapy supervisors succinctly told me the point of insight-oriented psychotherapy. Psychological defenses against reality work well only if they operate outside conscious awareness. Once you become aware of them and can see them operating, they lose much of their effectiveness. If you know that you are denying reality, it becomes more difficult to do so.

The same can be said of the mental distortions identified by cognitive therapists: they work best when we aren't paying attention. Once we know that we routinely engage in black-and-white thinking, the shades of grey slip into view. If we know we are catastrophizing, the milder and less melodramatic reality becomes apparent.

Similarly, we can develop an awareness of our own faulty wiring that gets activated when we search for comfort and fulfillment. By understanding our favored paths downward—and where they lead—we can catch ourselves before we set out. Failing this, we can notice when we are marching in the wrong direction. Rather than responding with confusion (*Wait—why isn't this working?*), we can sit back with amused recognition and gently turn ourselves around. *Ahh, right. You've been here before, old friend. Let's go the other way.*

The path upward is almost always more challenging to take than the descending route. The ladders are not so easy as the snakes. But the ladders lead to the sunlight and a lovely, expansive view.

SOME ADVICE, AT LAST

How can you make use of the material in this book? One method is to rate your own performance in recent years on the various misery-inducing strategies described in the preceding chapters. You might use a scale from 1 to 10, where 1 would mean "I never do this" and 10 would mean "I seem to do this constantly." Notice the items for which you give yourself more than 1 point. These are ways that you may inadvertently be serving your misery more than your best and happiest self.

Ask yourself what the upward path might look like. How could you get yourself onto it? For example, perhaps when life deals you a series of blows, you typically find yourself gorging on junk food—which serves only to make you feel ill and bloated. The temptation has been there in the past and will probably return next time as well. Rather than simply hoping that this doesn't happen, what could you do to intervene when it does?

You can also monitor your external stresses—the elements of life that are beyond your control—and make a point of taking note when they come at you too hard or too quickly. Knowing your attraction to junk food at such times, you could increase your vigilance for impulse purchases at the grocery store, making more of a point of keeping to your shopping list. You could buy snack food that will do you less harm or that you do not find quite so tempting. You could also give yourself permission to go out for fast food now and then—but perhaps not quite as often as your impulses might dictate.

In many cases, this will involve putting the brakes on the downhill slide. But you can also push yourself to turn around and move toward a happier state instead. You could make a point of taking time to cook healthy meals. You could ensure that you have a set of recipes, clearly bookmarked and accessible, that you know how to make. You could treat yourself to dinners out at restaurants that you know serve healthy food. And you could make yourself walk to them.

If, when feeling down, you notice that you compare yourself unfavorably against others more than usual (see lesson 23, "Measure Up and Measure Down"), use this knowledge. Knowing that you will be tempted to avoid social occasions, you could swim against the tide and push yourself to attend them instead. Maintain an awareness of the impulse to find high outliers (the best looking, the most successful, the funniest, the most knowledgeable) alongside whom you can make yourself feel deficient. Notice your mind searching them out. No need to chastise yourself for it. Take note of the characteristics (height? athletic ability? income?) that are most magnetic and potent.

Then, very deliberately, measure yourself against the entire group, not just that outlier. And give yourself permission to score in the bottom 10 percent on at least some variables without fleeing. To the degree you are able, turn the coin of envy over to its flip side: admiration. Forgive yourself for finding this difficult. Then do it again. These muscles, long unused, will protest at first but can strengthen with practice.

For each of your most prominent downward temptations, develop a plan to arrest the slide and turn in the opposite direction. Do not attempt to put these plans into effect all at once. Spreading your efforts across too many fronts is itself a trap. Work on no more than two or three tendencies at a time. When they become a bit easier (no one ever fully masters or erases them), take on new ones.

When you know there are temptations that are simply too powerful to resist, simply acknowledge the choice point that you are sliding past.

- *I know that isolating won't help.*

- *Someday I want to wear that bright purple outfit, but tonight I'm choosing the brown.*

- *I'm going along with this demand from my brother, but I do have the right to say no.*

Do so in an accepting manner. It is a choice. You have the right to make the choice you have made, and you have only so much strength to push for change. But by becoming increasingly aware of the fork in the road, you lay the groundwork for someday taking the other path. You can also feel less helpless in the face of your own negative emotions. *Well, I knew that watching television all night wasn't a solution, and it wasn't. I know that even more now.*

We will not eliminate negative emotion from our lives. Some pain is caused by our own actions or ways of thinking. Much is not.

A young intern I once supervised had led a fortunate life. She had never failed at anything significant. She had never attended a funeral. She had never been dumped. When she saw depressed people she found their despair hard to grasp. What was their problem? Life just didn't seem to be so difficult.

I took a page from therapists of the past and asked her what she most wanted for herself—what she would ask for if given a single selfish wish. She hesitated, but she agreed with my suggestion that she might ask for a long, long life with no significant illness. "A great wish," I said. "But notice what happens if it's granted. You will outlive everyone you ever loved. Your parents, siblings, your spouse, your children. Every home will fall into disrepair and decay. Having gained a long life, you will lose or bury everything that means anything to you. And that's what happens if you get your wish! If you don't, then everyone says goodbye to you instead, and you lose them anyway."

This, needless to say, she found a bit of a downer. But she could see that there is, behind all the joy and fun of life, an essential element of sadness and impermanence. Life is inherently difficult. Though it had not, as yet, been so for her, it would be eventually. None of us escapes that reality. We will feel sadness, grief, loss, fear, and every other challenging emotion.

But we will also live our lives in such a way as to make them more difficult and less fulfilling than they really need to be. This small book is designed to help identify some of the ways that we might do so. By becoming conscious of them, we may find it just a little bit easier to take the other road. Perhaps, as a result, the barriers that prevent us from fully developing our contributions to the world will become a little less daunting. I hope that you have found it useful.

Or maybe you were serious. You hopped this bus tour of hell genuinely hoping we would take you there. If so, good news: our tour has concluded. We have arrived. Please check your seats and take your belongings with you as you leave the bus. Stay as long as you like.

No need to put your coat on. It's warm out there.

Acknowledgments

This book arises from a talk I first gave at Psychology Salon, Changeways Clinic's lecture series for the public. Many thanks to the staff and organizers at Vancouver Public Library for hosting us. I would also like to thank the many participants at these talks who completed our surveys about the techniques they would use if, for some perverse reason, it was their goal to become unhappy.

My chief thanks in this book must go to my clients over the years, who have struggled mightily with a variety of concerns, chief among them clinical depression. They have shown the nature of true courage and have educated me much more than I have educated them. Their tolerance for somewhat unorthodox ideas, including the $10 Million Question, has been remarkable.

This strange project obviously runs the risk of trivializing depression and the very real pain that people experience. I hope that I have managed to make it absolutely clear that this is not my intent. We all find ourselves accidentally sabotaging our own happiness. Inevitably, my primary model for this tendency has been myself.

This book took shape against a backdrop of multiple conversations with friends and colleagues, including the psychologists at Changeways Clinic—Martha Capréol, Adrienne Wang, Anne Howson, Lindsey Thomas, Nancy Prober, Ekin Blackwell, Suja Srikameswaran, and Quincy-Robyn Young. Our clinic staff, chiefly Emily Wilson and Heather Cowie, held the fort, took over administration, juggled referrals, and organized talks and programs. Colleagues Dan Bilsker and Susan Mackey-Jamieson provided thoughts and feedback over dinner.

The great people at New Harbinger Publications have been extremely helpful in the preparation of the book. Thanks go to Melissa Kirk, Nicola Skidmore, Vicraj Gill, and Jennifer Eastman for their invaluable suggestions and tireless work on the manuscript. Thanks also to Michael Clark for his translation of lines from Dante's *Inferno*.

The book was written for the most part at a rural retreat in British Columbia. Many thanks to friends, relatives, and other guests who were tolerant enough to allow me to vanish for hours at a time. Yes, I heard the lawnmower and it was music to my ears. My chief support (and Buddhist encyclopedia), as with all of these writing projects, has been Geoff B, without whom the light might never shine.

Life has unexpected heartbreak and unpredictable joy. Some family members are with us from the beginning. Others appear on the journey. B, it was and is an honor.

Notes

1   A. A. Berlin, W. H. Kop, and P. A. Deuster, 2006. "Depressive Mood Symptoms and Fatigue After Exercise Withdrawal: The Potential Role of Decreased Fitness," *Psychosomatic Medicine* 68: 224–30.

2   J. A. Blumenthal et al., 1999, "Effects of Exercise Training on Older Patients with Major Depression," *Archives of Internal Medicine* 159: 2349–56.

3   NPD Group, 2010, *Gamer Segmentation 2010 Report*, May.

4   Alain de Botton, 2009, *The Pleasures and Sorrows of Work* (London: Penguin).

5   Dante Alighieri, *The Divine Comedy*, vol. 1, *Inferno*, canto 5, lines 121–23, trans. Michael Clark.

6   P. L. Hewitt and G. L. Flett, 1991, "Dimensions of Perfectionism in Unipolar Depression," *Journal of Abnormal Psychology* 100: 98–101.

7   United Nations, 2014, *World Urbanization Prospects: The 2014 Revision, Highlights*. Department of Economic and Social Affairs, Population Division.

8   Plutarch, 1920, *Lives*, vol. 9, *Pyrrhus*, 21.9.

References and Additional Reading

Abramson, L. Y., M. E. P. Seligman, and J. D. Teasdale. 1978. "Learned Helplessness in Humans: Critique and Reformulation." *Journal of Abnormal Psychology* 87: 49–74.

Alighieri, D. *The Divine Comedy*. Volume 1, *Inferno*.

Berlin, A. A., W. H. Kop, and P. A. Deuster. 2006. "Depressive Mood Symptoms and Fatigue after Exercise Withdrawal: The Potential Role of Decreased Fitness." *Psychosomatic Medicine* 68: 224–30.

Blumenthal, J. A., M. A. Babyak, K. A. Moore, W. E. Craighead, S. Herman, P. Khatri, et al. 1999. "Effects of Exercise Training on Older Patients with Major Depression." *Archives of Internal Medicine* 159: 2349–56.

Centre for Well-Being. 2012. *The Happy Planet Index: 2012 Report*. London: New Economics Foundation. http://www.happyplanetindex.org.

Crisp, Q. 1968. *The Naked Civil Servant*. New York: HarperCollins.

———. 1975. *How to Have a Lifestyle*. London: Cecil Woolf Publishers.

Currie, J. 2005. *The Marketization of Depression: The Prescribing of SSRI Antidepressants to Women*. Toronto: Women and Health Protection.

De Botton, A. 2004. *Status Anxiety*. London: Penguin.

———. 2009. *The Pleasures and Sorrows of Work*. London: Penguin.

Doll, R., R. Peto, J. Boreham, and I. Sutherland. 2004. "Mortality in Relation to Smoking: 50 Years' Observations on Male British Doctors." *British Medical Journal* 328: 1519.

Ehrenreich, B. 2009. *Bright Sided: How Positive Thinking Is Undermining America*. New York: Metropolitan Books.

Ferguson, W. 2002. *Happiness*. Toronto: Penguin Canada.

Fredrickson, B. 2009. *Positivity*. New York: Crown.

Gilbert, D. 2006. *Stumbling on Happiness*. New York: Random House.

Healy, D. 2004. *Let Them Eat Prozac: The Unhealthy Relationship Between the Pharmaceutical Industry and Depression*. New York: New York University Press.

Hewitt, P. L., and G. L. Flett. 1991. "Dimensions of Perfectionism in Unipolar Depression." *Journal of Abnormal Psychology* 100: 98–101.

Hollis, J. 1993. *The Middle Passage: From Misery to Meaning in Midlife*. Toronto: Inner City Books.

Kirsch, I. 2009. *The Emperor's New Drugs: Exploding the Antidepressant Myth*. London: The Bodley Head.

Koerner, K., and M. M. Linehan. 2011. *Doing Dialectical Behavior Therapy: A Practical Guide*. New York: Guilford.

Lewis, C. S. 1946. *The Great Divorce*. New York: The Macmillan Company.

Nielsen Company. 2013. *Free to Move Between Screens: The Cross-Platform Report, March 2013*. New York: The Nielsen Company.

NPD Group. 2010. *Gamer Segmentation 2010 Report*. May.

Otto, M., and J. Smits. 2011. *Exercise for Mood and Anxiety: Proven Strategies for Overcoming Depression and Enhancing Well-Being*. New York: Oxford University Press.

Paterson, R. 2000. *The Assertiveness Workbook: How to Express Your Ideas and Stand Up for Yourself at Work and in Relationships*. Oakland CA: New Harbinger Publications.

Plutarch. 1920. *Lives*. Vol. 9, *Demetrius and Antony; Pyrrhus and Caius Marius*. Translated by B. Perrin. Cambridge, MA: Harvard University Press.

Pratt, L. A., D. J. Brody, and Q. Gu. 2011. *Antidepressant Use in Persons Aged 12 and Over: United States, 2005–2008*. NCHS data brief, no 76. Hyattsville, MD: National Center for Health Statistics.

Putnam, R. D. 2000. *Bowling Alone: The Collapse and Revival of American Community*. New York: Simon & Schuster.

Sartre, J.-P. 1989. *No Exit and Three Other Plays*. New York: Vintage.

Savage, D. 1998. *Savage Love: Straight Answers from America's Most Popular Sex Columnist*. New York: Plume.

United Nations. 2014. *World Urbanization Prospects: The 2014 Revision, Highlights*. Department of Economic and Social Affairs, Population Division.

World Health Organization. 2008. *The Global Burden of Disease: 2004 Update*. Geneva: World Health Organization.

Randy J. Paterson, PhD, is director of Changeways Clinic, a private psychology practice in Vancouver, BC, Canada. He is author of *The Assertiveness Workbook* and *Your Depression Map*, and conducts training programs for professionals on evidence-based treatment. Through Changeways Clinic, Paterson presents lectures and workshops internationally on topics including mental health policy, cognitive behavioral therapy (CBT), the nature and treatment of depression and anxiety disorders, and strategies for private practice management. He is the 2008 recipient of the Canadian Psychological Association's Distinguished Practitioner Award. For more information on Paterson, his presentations and workshops, or Changeways Clinic, visit www .randypaterson.com. To view Paterson's blog on psychological and practice issues, please visit www.psychologysalon.com.

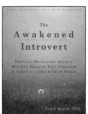
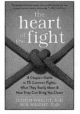